Our Scots NOBLE FAMILIES.

By THOMAS JOHNSTON
(Editor of "FORWARD")

WITH PREFACE
BY
J. RAMSAY MACDONALD, M.P.

& INTRODUCTION
TO THIS NEW EDITION
BY
BRIAN D. OSBORNE

© Mary B. Knox

© Introduction to this edition Brian D. Osborne

First Published 1909
"Forward" Publishing Co., Ltd.
164 Howard St. Glasgow

This edition 1999, Reprinted 2001
Argyll Publishing
Glendaruel
Argyll PA22 3AE

**British Library Cataloguing-in-Publication Data.
A catalogue record for this book is available from
the British Library.**

ISBN 1 902831 01 2

Typeset & Origination
Cordfall Ltd, Glasgow

Printing & Binding
Bell & Bain Ltd, Glasgow

CONTENTS.

Publisher's Note

This new edition is produced in the style of the original. Only minimal editing – mainly on inaccuracies – has been done. Some typesetting and spelling conventions may seem archaic and the reader should note, for example, that the older spelling of Dumbartonshire is used both by Tom Johnston and by Brian Osborne in his introduction. The form Dunbartonshire was introduced only after World War I.

INTRODUCTION

TO THIS NEW EDITION.

WHEN THE Rt. Hon. Thomas Johnston, Privy Councillor, Companion of Honour, died in 1965 there was a general recognition that one of the great Scottish figures of the twentieth century had gone from the land. His career had indeed been distinguished – a junior ministerial post and then cabinet office under Ramsay MacDonald, spoken of as a potential leader of the Labour Party in the 1930s, an outstanding Secretary of State for Scotland in the war-time coalition under Churchill, a possible choice by Clement Attlee as the last Viceroy of India, and a host of post-war public appointments.

At first glance little links the distinguished veteran who had so dominated Scottish public life for most of this century with the radical young journalist whose exposé of the reprehensible past and questionable present of much of the Scottish aristocracy in *Our Scots Noble Families* proved a controversial bestseller in 1909. However, the young firebrand and the elder statesman shared a passionate love for Scotland and a desire to see its land and people prosper. Johnston's concern is as much about mismanagement of the land and oppression of the people as it is about privilege and peculation.

Tom Johnston (the form of his name by which he was universally known – although he signed letters, wrote articles and published books as the more formal Thomas Johnston) was born in the small Dumbartonshire town of Kirkintilloch on 2nd

November 1881 to a modest middle-class background. His parents kept a small grocer's shop, an uncle was a lawyer, another relative owned a small printing and publishing business in Glasgow. Johnston was not, in contrast to many of his later 'Red Clydeside' contemporaries, from a working class background.

After completing his education, at Kirkintilloch's Lairdsland School and Lenzie Academy, a very brief trial of life in his lawyer uncle's office convinced him that a legal career was not for him, and he took a number of clerical posts in the local iron-founding industry and in insurance before persuading his mother's cousin to entrust him with the management of his printing works and the two weekly papers it produced.

In 1911, aged 29, he successfully stood for election on the Independent Labour Party ticket for a School Board election in Kirkintilloch. For some reason Johnston later wrote that he served on the School Board from 1903, just after his 21st birthday. In any event this seemingly modest arena for political activity soon saw the exercise of Johnston's characteristic energy and imagination. As the junior member of the Board he was given the Convenership of the least desirable and least significant Committee – that dealing with evening classes. Kirkintilloch's evening classes were not well attended and, in consequence, only attracted a low level of government grant aid. Johnston hit upon the ingenious notion of encouraging attendances by offering a free place at a dancing class, to be held in a local public hall, to any young person who could demonstrate regular attendance at one of the Board's more orthodox educational classes. The dancing classes attracted crowds and the uptake of the Board's classes in mathematics, mining, and English increased in like measure.

More serious issues attracted Johnston's attention. Spurred on by his enthusiasm the Board did pioneering work on the feeding of poor children attending their schools. In 1912 he stood for election to Kirkintilloch Town Council, but failed to win a place. However the next year saw him elected to the Council on which he served until 1921, by which time national politics had claimed his services. Kirkintilloch, largely inspired by Johnston, developed a reputation for Municipal Socialism. An early example was the creation of a civic entertainments programme, covering everything from lectures to operatic recitals in the park, all funded from the profits of a Municipal Cinema whose prices were set to undercut the commercial cinemas of Glasgow – eight miles to the south. Municipal kitchens, municipal pig farms and even municipal jam-making all flourished under Johnston's guidance.

A more complex undertaking came in 1920 when Johnston, then Convener of the Council's Finance Committee, persuaded his colleagues to establish the Kirkintilloch Municipal Bank Ltd. Floated on a loan from the town's Common Good Fund, and underwritten by the Scottish Co-operative Wholesale Society, the Bank was run by Council employees as part of their normal duties, with the Burgh Treasurer as Bank Manager. Add to this a series of campaigns to improve the deplorable state of much of the town's privately rented housing and it will become clear why Kirkintilloch attracted attention as a progressive and interventionist burgh. Temperance was a major issue for Johnston and many of his socialist contemporaries and largely through his advocacy of the measure Kirkintilloch voted, by means of local veto polls, to withdraw all public house licenses and go 'dry', a policy which prevailed from 1920 to 1968.

In 1906, established in the Springburn offices of his printing company, the 24 year old Johnston found himself responsible for a weekly local newspaper, *The St Rollox & Springburn Express* and a weekly journal, *Scots Commercial Record*, devoted to the grocery trade and incidentally extremely hostile to the Co-operative movement. Having a printing press at his command Johnston decided that he would create a Scottish Socialist weekly and on Saturday 13th October 1906 *Forward*, ambitiously subtitled 'A Scots Weekly Journal of Socialism, Trade Unionism, and

Democratic Thought', was launched. One penny bought 8 pages of news and opinion about national and international developments, socialist activities, organisations and issues.

In the first issue Johnston set out his motives in characteristically vivid terms. Entitled 'Why we came' his editorial explained:

> We came 'cause we had to. Our coming, is we believe, at the psychological moment. For many years the massed forces of reaction, the pimps, the plunderers, the conservers, the old women in trousers, the farthing reformers, have had it all their own way. A Capitalist press, from the 'Scotsman' in Edinburgh to the 'News' and the 'Record' in Glasgow, consistently and with one accord, stifles, throttles, jeers, misrepresents, and caricatures the wailing shriek of the underdog for Justice.

The first number covered women's issues and the temperance question as well as the more narrowly party political material. Johnston himself contributed an article on access to the countryside on the estates of the Duke of Montrose – perhaps the seeds of *Our Scots Noble Families* can be found here. An account of the Labour Movement in Ayrshire was perhaps predictable enough but the eclectic range of the new journal was demonstrated by an article on 'Why Socialists should study Spiritualism'. Advertising was, as ever for left wing journals, something of a problem and *Forward* relied on advertising from a few sympathetic companies and a broad sweep of progressive organisations. The first issue carried advertisements from the Scottish Secular Society, the Scottish Vegetarian Society, local ILP branches and the 'Arcadian' Food Reform Restaurant.

Johnston wrote extensively for the journal and also used the publishing company to bring out more substantial works such as his 1907 pamphlet *The Case for Women's Suffrage*. The appallingly unhealthy working conditions at the Shawfield Chemical Works in Glasgow were the subject of a fierce attack in April

1907 in an issue which saw contributions from Keir Hardie, MP. Johnston and *Forward* were, from the outset, able to attract a wide range of contributors from among the Scottish socialist pioneers such as Keir Hardie, as well as national figures such as Shaw and H.G. Wells.

The columns of *Forward* were also open to the opposition – in November 1907 Lord Balfour of Burleigh, a former Tory Secretary of State for Scotland, was given most of a page to explain 'Why I disagree with Socialism and why I fought the Feeding of Schoolchildren Bill'. Lord Balfour was, of course, answered, Johnston contributing an editorial rebuttal and continuing the argument over three quarters of a page in the following week. Balfour came back with a counter-argument and a long letter by him appeared in a December 1907 issue.

Forward although 'A Scots Weekly Journal' was by no means parochial. In June 1907 Johnston wrote 'What anarchism and nihilism mean – Prince Kropotkin's escape from prison' – an account of the adventures of the Russian anarchist and revolutionary Prince Peter Kropotkin – and around this time *Forward* also carried a series of articles on Buddhism.

In February 1908 *Forward* ran an article on the Vatersay land raiders – the campaign by Barra cottars to obtain land on the neighbouring island of Vatersay to develop crofts – and the hostile reaction of the Gordons of Barra, who owned both islands. The land question, particularly in the Highlands and Islands, had been an active one for many years. The plight of Highland communities had been investigated by the Napier Commission, appointed in 1883, and the Crofters Act of 1886 gave crofters security of tenure, fixed rents, the right to inherit and bequeath the croft and compensation for improvements. However there was an inadequate supply of crofting land in many areas and estates often proved unwilling to make over sheep runs or to release sporting ground for crofting purposes. Vatersay was a case in point, being occupied by one tenanted sheep-farm. A

Congested Districts Board had been established in 1897 to acquire land for leasing to crofters, but, as the Vatersay experience demonstrated, with only limited success. In 1909 the Board, however, succeeded in purchasing Vatersay and divided it into 58 crofting tenures.

The national political climate of the period also put the great aristocratic land-owning families centre stage. The 1906 General Election had seen a Liberal landslide (and the election of 26 candidates supported by the Labour Representation Committee – the origins of the Labour Party.) The new Prime Minister, Henry Campbell-Bannerman, and more particularly his successor from 1908, Herbert Asquith, planned a more active social policy than earlier Liberal premiers. As a signal of this change Chancellor of the Exchequer David Lloyd George introduced an Old Age Pensions bill in 1908. Conservative opposition to Government measures in the House of Commons was easily outvoted by the Liberal and Labour forces but the blocking potential of the House of Lords with its in-built Tory majority of hereditary peers presented a major obstacle to the Government. An example of this had been the repeated defeat of the Small Landholders (Scotland) Bill. This measure, to improve on the tenancy arrangements in the 1886 Crofters' Holdings Act and to create a Board of Agriculture for Scotland, replacing the Crofters Commission and the Congested Districts Board, had passed the Commons with a large majority but was defeated in the Lords in 1907 and 1908.

The land question became a major political issue throughout Britain, though nowhere more actively pursued than in Scotland. Crowded meetings discussed the issue and joined in singing the 'Liberal Land Song':

> *The land! The land! 'Twas God who gave the land!*
> *The land! The land! The ground on which we stand!*
> *Why should we be beggars with the ballot in our hand?*
> *God gave the land to the people!*

When Lloyd George introduced the so-called People's Budget in 1909, with increased taxes on tobacco and alcohol, increased rates of income tax, and a nationwide duty on increased land values payable on the transfer of property, he provoked, or perhaps more accurately, engineered a major confrontation with the Upper House. This struggle ran on for two years, through two general elections and was finally only resolved by the threat to create enough Liberal Peers to force the measures through the Lords. The Parliament Act of 1911 reduced the delaying power of the House of Lords to two years, and to only one month in the case of money Bills.

In all of this controversy between a popularly elected (albeit on a restricted franchise) House of Commons and an unelected House of Lords a significant part of the argument focused on the legitimacy of a hereditary peerage exercising such powers. The House of Lords claimed that they represented a stabilising and traditional force which could properly tame the wilder excesses of popular democracy, such as land value taxation, measures that the Peerage saw as exploitation, theft and robbery.

Tom Johnston aimed to show that the aristocracy had only reached their present state of power and privilege by exploitation, theft and robbery on the grandest of scales. As he wrote in his introduction to *Our Scots Noble Families* – 'A General Indictment':

> . . . today, In Scotland, our artisans and peasants appear to believe that these ancient noble families hold their privileges and lands at the earnest behest of Divine Providence; that their wealth has been justly earned; and that their titles are but rewards for honest service to the State.
>
> The first step in Reform, either of the Land Laws or of the House of Lords, is to destroy these superstitions. Show the people that our Old Nobility is not noble; that its lands are stolen lands – stolen either by force or fraud, show people that the title-deeds are rapine, murder, massacre, cheating, or Court harlotry;

> dissolve the halo of divinity that surrounds the hereditary title. . .

His first step in this process was the publication in *Forward*, from June 1908, of a series of articles under the heavily ironic series title 'Our "Noble" Families'. Johnston's first target was one of Scotland's largest landowners, the Dukes of Atholl. In July he moved on to the Gordons of Barra, the landowners involved in the Vatersay land raid, and in August to the family most notoriously associated with the Highland Clearances – the Sutherlands. In July 1909 the time was seen as ripe for the publication of the series of articles in book form as *Our Scots Noble Families*, although the cover used the shorter and less accurate title *Our Noble Families* (a title by which it is often cited). An advertisement in *Forward* claimed:

> This is Democracy's first real attack on Scots Landowners and Privilege-mongers. Thirty-five Noble families, their origin, their history, their plunder. Thirty-five coronets in the Dock. Gives us for the first time the real history of Scotland.

Johnston's aim was not dispassionate analysis, he aimed to provide a weapon for a political campaign. Ramsay MacDonald, who had been elected to Parliament in 1906, and would become leader of the Labour Party, in succession to Keir Hardie, in 1911 and the first Labour Prime Minister in 1924, contributed a foreword which underlined the book's aim. In it he said:

> The story of the people in history is the best handbook for the guidance of the people in politics.

MacDonald's point was echoed in the *Forward* advertisement which described *Our Scots Noble Families* as 'the *vade mecum* of the Scots Land Reformer'.

The publication of *Our Scots Noble Families* was not Johnston's only contribution to the land question. In 1909 a new Highland Land League was formed, with Johnston as Vice

President, and with a strong link to the Labour Party. Johnston advocated buying out landowners and creating more crofting holdings to satisfy demand for land in the Highlands and to reverse the depopulation of the area. It was, throughout his career, one of his major concerns to keep the problems of rural areas on the agenda of a largely urban-based and urban-focused Scottish Labour movement. He wrote in *Forward* in September 1909 about the Land League:

> The only hope of the working class is definite and clear cut organisation for political and economic ends; and these ends must include the State ownership of land, and the great means of production. The crofters and cottars have everything to gain and nothing to lose by allying themselves with the working class of the towns, and the working class of the towns has everything to gain by alliance with the crofters.

Our Scots Noble Families was criticised on political grounds, and on grounds of taste, but Johnston's exhaustive historical research stood up to the closest scrutiny. Much of the information on land ownership was derived from official Parliamentary Papers published in 1872-73 'The Return of Owners of Land: Scotland', while his accounts of the rise and activities of his 'Noble Families' came from works such as the First and Second Statistical Accounts, Burke's 'Peerage' and the nineteenth century family histories which had been written about many of his subjects. Johnston's sources were thus standard ones, open to verification, although his interpretations and his polemical style were very much his own and would doubtless have shocked many of the douce clergymen and antiquarians who, unwittingly, had furnished him with his ammunition.

The principle on which Johnston selected his families to study is rather difficult to determine. On the Keiths he finds little to say after the sixteenth century and the Boyles do not, he notes appear to have been 'engaged in notorious theft or scandalous murder'. Equally some noted names are not included

– the Highland chiefs associated with the Clearances, for example, seem somewhat under-represented.

Johnston looked at the ways in which his subjects had risen to power and prosperity, he examined their land holdings, their record in land management and he also often brought matters down to the present day. Discussing the Bruces he continued his earlier sparring in the columns of *Forward* with Lord Balfour of Burleigh, a scion of the House of Bruce. He noted:

> Lord Burleigh draws £100 a month, having as an ex-Cabinet Minister signed a plea that he was too poor to do without some State help. This pension does not, however, seem to have destroyed his energies or his capacity for thrift, for he 'directs' some 7 public Companies (total capital over £88,000,000), engaged in banking, rails, steamships and telegraphs. In his spare time he amuses himself with the pleasantries of the Anti-Socialist League, endeavouring to revive antediluvian political theories. He was wildly excited over the introduction of an old-age pension of five shillings per week to working class octogenarians, believing that State pensions destroy self-reliance and individuality. He left us to infer that he spoke from personal experience.

The passion and wit with which Johnston attacked his subjects made *Our Scots Noble Families* a bestseller. In all it would sell 120,000 copies and go through nine editions between 1909 and 1918. Its success seems hardly to have been hindered by the refusal 'for political reasons' of John Menzies, Scotland's largest wholesale newsagent, to stock or distribute it.

By July and August 1909 *Forward* was able to include in its publicity for the book comment from other journals and from leading political figures. The socialist aristocrat Robert Bontine Cunninghame Graham (whose family had not escaped Johnston's pen) declared that Johnston's articles 'are very well done', while the Liberal newspaper the *Morning Leader* stated 'We commend this book very heartily'. Perhaps equally interesting was the reaction from the Conservative press. It was, Glasgow's *Evening Times* conceded, 'as an *ex-parte* statement, undoubtedly clever' while a brief review in the Tory *Glasgow News* managed, in fifty words, to pack in a series of put-downs, remove the subject from its contemporary context and grudgingly acknowledge the force of Johnston's writing:

> A brochure dealing 'faithfully' with the history of our aristocratic Scottish families – their murders, treacheries, and above-all their land-grabbings. Mr Johnston's delvings into ancient history are not uninteresting, but he writes with strongly marked animus – and, after all, most of it is admittedly ancient history by this time.

The 'strongly marked animus' can hardly be missed. Johnston, indeed, came to regret some of the tone and content of *Our Scots Noble Families*. Writing in his autobiography, *Memories*, published in 1952, the now ex-politician described his articles as:

> . . . a rather pungent and scurrilous series of tracts purporting to be the undercover – or almost undercover – record of the great landowning families in Scotland.

He goes on to say:

> . . . there were at least some descriptions in my collected tracts . . . which were historically one-sided and unjust and quite unnecessarily wounding.

Emrys Hughes, who succeeded Johnston as editor of *Forward*, however was of the opinion that the young Johnston was nearer to the truth than the old Johnston.

Many authors have regretted their juvenilia, few have done so with quite such vigour as Johnston. In later life, on his travels around Scotland, he visited second hand book shops and systematically bought up copies of *Our Scots Noble Families*. When asked by a member of his staff at the Hydro Board why he did this he remarked, 'times have changed'.

There is no doubt that as Johnston's political career developed *Our Scots Noble Families* became for him an acute embarrassment. Johnston attributed the fact that when he was proposed, by two impeccably Conservative Members of Parliament, for membership of the Caledonian Club in London in the 1930s, he was blackballed due to continuing aristocratic resentment at his treatment of the 'noble families'. It is significant that Johnston allowed his equally fiery, if less personally directed, *History of the Working Classes in Scotland*, published in 1920, to be reprinted on a number of occasions, down to 1946, while *Our Scots Noble Families*, despite its high sales, was allowed to go out of print.

Forward continued to flourish. Johnston's opposition to the First World War – a conflict which he described as:

> . . . a cause in which we have no interest, in which we were never consulted, and from which by no conceivable result can we derive any advantage. . .

led him into conflict with the Government, and in particular with the Minister of Munitions, David Lloyd George. One issue which *Forward* took up was Government control of conditions in munitions factories and the employment of 'dilutees', unskilled and swiftly trained men and women brought in to augment skilled workers. Lloyd George came to Glasgow to address a workers rally in December 1915 and found a noisily hostile audience unwilling to be seduced by the famed Lloyd George charm.

Forward gleefully printed a report of the Minister's reception and suffered the consequences of a police raid, confiscation of the offending issue and a temporary ban. After five weeks *Forward* agreed not to cause disaffection over the Munitions of War Act or the dilutees issue and was back on the streets; back with a 10,000 increase in circulation as a result of the publicity the case had attracted. Johnston was later to describe the Government's action as giving *Forward* thousands of pounds worth of free advertising.

By the end of the war in 1918 Johnston was a leading figure in Scottish Labour politics and, urged on by James Maxton, was adopted as the Independent Labour Party candidate for West Stirlingshire in the 1918 General Election. The wartime Prime Minister, Lloyd George, was seeking re-election at the head of a Liberal and Conservative & Unionist Coalition. Lloyd George's decision to fight alongside the Conservatives split his party and in West Stirlingshire the electorate was faced with a Coalition Candidate, Harry Hope; an anti-Coalition Liberal, none other than R.B.Cunninghame Graham in one of his many political manifestations, and Johnston. Johnston was beaten into a poor second place by the Coalition candidate.

When the Coalition collapsed in 1922 and another General Election was fought on more clearly defined party lines, Johnston again stood for West Stirlingshire and, in a straight contest with the Conservative Hope, Johnston won 52% of the vote.

Johnston went to Westminster in 1922 with a remarkable group of Labour members from the West of Scotland – John Wheatley, James Maxton, David Kirkwood, Emmanuel Shinwell were just some of the Clydesiders who were to form part of the 142 strong Parliamentary Labour Party under Ramsay MacDonald. Johnston was soon to cut a significant figure at Westminster – his political skills and energy were complemented by good looks and a taste for smart clothes. Johnston's trademark bow-tie marked him out from many of his colleagues whose minds were above such sartorial refinements.

The retirement of the Conservative Premier Bonar Law and his replacement by Baldwin brought about a policy change on Free Trade and Protection and an unexpected General

Election in 1923. The Conservatives continued in office without an overall majority but in January 1924 Stanley Baldwin resigned and Ramsay MacDonald formed the first Labour government. Despite his prominence in Labour politics Johnston was not included in MacDonald's first administration. The balance of forces in Westminster was such that a long life could not be expected for the minority Labour Government and in November 1924 MacDonald was obliged to go to the country. This election saw the publication of the forged Zinoviev letter, linking the Labour administration to the Soviet government. Conservative newspapers played up the 'Red Scare' and the Conservative Party swept back into power. Among the many Labour casualties was Johnston in West Stirlingshire.

However his standing in the Labour movement ensured a swift return to Westminster and a by-election just a few weeks after the General Election saw him elected for Dundee, which he represented until the 1929 General Election when, because of internal political dissent in the constituency, he returned to contest his old, and more local seat, of West Stirlingshire. Elected with a handsome majority he found himself, for the first time, part of the largest single party in the House. MacDonald was invited by King George V to form an administration and this time he included Johnston as Parliamentary Under-secretary in the Scottish Office.

Johnston enjoyed the varied work which came the way of a Scottish Office minister but in March 1931 he was promoted to Cabinet rank and given the non-departmental post of Lord Privy Seal and assigned responsibility for the Government's programme to tackle unemployment. His time in this post was limited. A financial crisis brought down the Labour Government in August 1931 and while Ramsay MacDonald went on to split his party by forming a National Government, Johnston, like most of his Cabinet colleagues, left office.

At the 1931 General Election Johnston suffered in the general Labour collapse and lost his seat. The leadership of the Parliamentary Labour Party fell vacant and of course Johnston was unable to contest it.

He fought a by-election in his home county of Dumbarton-shire in March 1932. This was contested by a Conservative (on the National Government ticket), a Communist, a Scottish Nationalist and Johnston. Ironically, in the light of Johnston's long-standing and vigorous support for Scottish devolution, the intervention of the Nationalist candidate probably cost him the seat.

In 1933 Johnston finally gave up the editorship of *Forward*, although his deputy, Emrys Hughes, had been acting as editor while Johnston was in government or on parliamentary duty in London. Johnston continued as chairman of the *Forward* publishing company and continued to write feature articles for the journal. At the 1935 General Election Johnston fought what proved to be his last campaign and was returned as member for West Stirlingshire & Clackmannan and again took up the role of an opposition Member of Parliament.

On the outbreak of war in 1939 Johnston accepted the post of Regional Commissioner for Civil Defence in Scotland. In this role he dealt with the evacuation of children from the cities, air raid precautions, food and rationing and the formation of a National Fire Service. One of the intriguing consequences of this appointment was that Johnston had as his deputes, firstly Lord Airlie (whose family had for some reason escaped treatment in *Our Scots Noble Families*) and then Lord Rosebery (who most certainly had not escaped the Johnston touch.)

In February 1941 Winston Churchill invited Johnston to join the wartime National Government as Secretary of State for Scotland. Johnston accepted, on condition that he could form a Council of State for Scotland, comprising all the ex-Secretaries of State, and if they agreed on a Scottish issue Churchill would back them. Through the medium of this Council of State Johnston was able to lay the foundations for post-war reconstruction long before the certainty of winning the war was assured. Housing, herring fisheries, health, hill sheep farming, economic development, town & country planning – all fell under the consideration of Johnston and his Council.

Among the most notable achievements of Johnston's period of office was the creation of the North of Scotland Hydro Electric Board, a body given the dual remit of generating and distributing electricity from Highland water power and encouraging the social and economic well-being of the Highlands. Johnston modelled his plan for the Hydro Board on the success of the Tennessee Valley Authority, created under Franklin Roosevelt's New Deal programme.

In 1937 Johnston had advised his constituency party that he did not wish to fight the next General Election, due by 1940. As a result of the war the election never took place and Johnston served until the end of the National Government and the General Election of 1945.

Both Churchill, in his dissolution Honours List, and Attlee, on taking office, offered Johnston a seat in the House of Lords, an offer which he refused, as later he was to refuse the Order of the Thistle because it would have meant using the title 'Sir'. He did accept, from Churchill in 1953, appointment as a Companion of Honour, an order carrying no title and only signified by the letters C.H. after the bearer's name.

In 1945 Johnston was 63 years of age, active, vigorous and as convinced as ever that he had much to offer his country. Retirement was not an option. He was appointed as Chairman of his own creation, the Hydro Board, a post which he held for thirteen years of enormous activity and progress. He was also appointed to the Forestry Commission and chaired the

Commission's Scottish Committee. Both these roles brought him into regular contact with Highland and Lowland landowners – with all the potential embarrassment over the forty year old, but still wounding, *Our Scots Noble Families*.

During Johnston's spell as Under Secretary at the Scottish Office he had become interested in the potential of tourism as an agency for the development of Scotland. In December 1945 the Scottish Tourist Board was formed, with Johnston as its first Chairman, a post he was to occupy for over nine years. In 1955 he was appointed as Chairman of the Broadcasting Council for Scotland and a Governor of the BBC.

Johnston died at his home in Milngavie, six miles from his birthplace in Kirkintilloch on 5th September 1965 aged 83. The *Scotsman* commented that he was:

> . . . the greatest Scotsman of modern times and the one who did most for his country.

This was a view that was widely echoed. The *Glasgow Herald* printed a lengthy obituary and also reflected on Johnston's place in history in its Leader Column:

> It was not the least of Tom Johnston's achievements that he was the most outstanding Secretary of State for Scotland in this century.

It went on to reflect on the character of the man:

> Pre-eminently he was a Scot, but to the austere Scottish characteristics he added charm and humour. All his passionate concern for his own country was saved by these last virtues from degenerating into embittered nationalism. But he undoubtedly was a nationalist figure. Unlike many of his contemporaries in the Scottish Labour movement he did not allow his Lowland industrial origins to dictate the direction of his political intentions. It was no accident that his greatest achievements lay outside the traditional area

of Labour activity, in agriculture and the Highlands. He leaves a reputation for devotion to Scottish affairs which won an equally generous response from his countrymen.

Tom Johnston's place in history is secure. The fate of *Our Scots Noble Families* may seem less certain. The *Glasgow News* reviewer in 1909 felt that the events related were 'ancient history by this time'. How much more ancient must they be ninety years later when the issues that lay behind Johnston's tract must surely have been resolved by the passage of so many years and so much legislation.

Well perhaps not. The reform of the House of Lords is still a topical and contentious issue. The struggle of the Assynt crofters, the islanders of Eigg and the inhabitants of Knoydart to gain some measure of control over the land on which they live and work has filled many a newspaper column in the 1990s – just as the struggle of the Vatersay land raiders did in the first decade of the twentieth century, or the Crofters' War did in the 1880s. Access to the countryside, the subject of Johnston's first *Forward* column, is as lively an issue at the end of the century as it was at the beginning. Johnston's target was the traditional aristocratic landowner, but it is hard to imagine that he would have viewed the passing of vast tracts of Scotland into the hands of absentee landowners with equanimity.

Johnston noted that in the 1891 the rural areas of Scotland had a population of 928,513 – a figure which was reduced by 1901 to 885,809. A startling example of this change is revealed by the population figures for the seven crofting counties (Argyll, Inverness, Ross & Cromarty, Sutherland, Caithness, Orkney & Shetland). When Johnston was born these seven counties had a total population of 369,453. By the time of his death this total had fallen to 277,716 – a decline of over 91,000. Perhaps more striking is the fact that these counties, which in 1881 had accounted for 9.9% of the total Scottish population, by the 1961 Census only represented 5.4% of the population.

Johnston's comment in *Our Scots Noble Families* rings true:

> These figures tell the story of the strangulation of a
> race; they tell us that the Celt is being slowly, if silently,
> cleared from the croft of his fathers, and that soon
> no sound will echo in the smiling valleys but the crack
> of the sportsman's rifle and the plaintive cry of the
> lonely whaup. So long as half a dozen families own
> one-half of Scotland, so long will countless families
> own none of it. . .

We are, today, accustomed to think of the Highlands as an empty landscape and somehow assume that this is the natural order of things. Just as the treeless deer forests and grouse moors are a man-made construct so is a depopulated glen. It is significant that the Government body established at the end of the nineteenth century to provide additional crofting land was called the Congested Districts Board. The notion of 'congested districts' in the Highlands now seems strange but Ross and Cromarty alone declined in population by 27% between 1881 and 1961 – a loss of over 20,000 people in a period when Scotland's population grew by almost 39%.

The vein of social inquiry which Johnston opened up into land ownership and land management has developed since his day. There is perhaps now less concern about the hereditary nature of land ownership and more concern about how land is bought and sold, how land is managed and how social control is exercised.

John McEwen's *Who Owns Scotland*, first published in 1977, which examined the contemporary structure of land ownership testifies to the survival skills of the great traditional landowners; the famous names that appear in *Our Scots Noble Families* appear in *Who Owns Scotland* – Argyll and Atholl, Buccleuch and Roxburghe still ring through the list of major landowners despite claims of a century of confiscation and penal taxation. Johnston said, when asked why he bought up copies of *Our Scots Noble*

Families, 'times have changed'. Perhaps they have changed less than Johnston thought although McEwen chronicles the decline of traditional estates in Perthshire and comments:

> . . . one of the terrible features of land-ownership not only in Perthshire but all over Scotland, is that our most precious asset can be played about with in some gambling den, or as a result of family feuds, with the consequence that the land is abused and the rural communities perish.

More recent studies such as Andy Wightman's *Who Owns Scotland* and Auslan Cramb's *Who Owns Scotland Now; the use and abuse of private land* build on McEwen's work. Auslan Cramb, in particular, looked beyond the mechanics of land ownership to examine in detail the impact different styles of land ownership and land management have on communities. He gives examples of enlightened foreign landowners, progressive traditional landowners and examples of land ownership which are much less acceptable. Cramb points out that while many European countries have restrictions on the purchase of land by foreign owners at least 500,000 acres of Scotland are owned by offshore companies and foreign interests.

There must surely be, in the context of a Scottish Parliament, an informed debate as to whether it is reasonable to accept that the ownership of land and the massive impact that this can have on the life and livelihood of people living on the land should be entirely left to chance and the play of market forces. The chance of land being owned by the nth generation of an aristocratic family, the chance of land being bought and sold by an industrial company (as was the fate of Knoydart), the chance of land being bought by an absentee landlord with no interest in it outwith the fishing, grouse-shooting or deer-stalking seasons, the chance of land being bought by a foreign owner out of sympathy with Scottish customs and attitudes have all proved equally problematic. Foreign owners and traditional lairds have indeed proved to be diligent and caring trustees of the land – but this too has been chance.

As this debate unfolds Tom Johnston's *Our Scots Noble Families* will rightfully take its place as a seminal work in the literature of land reform and land ownership.

BRIAN D. OSBORNE
KIRKINTILLOCH
JANUARY 1999

PREFACE.

House of Commons.

MR. JOHNSTON has done me the honour to ask me to write a few introductory sentences to his book, and I comply with pleasure, for I welcome the publication of these studies with great heartiness.

I am writing in the midst of Budget debates, and I have to listen day after day to representatives of the class dealt with in these chapters, describing the Budget as exploitation, theft, and robbery; and day after day answer is made to them in the form of an apology. The state of national finance, the richness of the rich, and the poverty of the poor, the necessity of maintaining Free Trade—upon such lines are the answers couched, and thus the upholders of the Budget seem to depreciate their own virtues and sound finance, and apologise for every blow they deal. That is making their success difficult.

This will occur every time the State resumes a part of social values. It is, therefore, necessary to make it clear to the public that we are not, on such occasions, to stand on the defensive, but to assume the offensive. The origin of the classes must be inquired into. By what manner of means did they acquire their broad acres ? How have money-lenders become peers, and merchants, princes ? When they stick "robber" on the back of everyone who votes in support of this Budget, what is their title to pose as honest men ? Mr. Johnston has supplied part of the answer. I need refer to but one instance, and I will take the Campbells of Blythswood, because they afford the most typical example of the matter under consideration. They were Provosts of Glasgow, and Glasgow had common lands. Being Provosts, they had special facilities for acquiring these lands. Without purchase or compensation, which amounted to more than half-a-farthing per square yard, they got possession of close upon two million square yards of that common property. To-day, they subscribe to the Constitution, and to honest politics, and their moral nature is shocked because the Budget taxes them. They are convinced that Justice no longer rules in this country. They have broken their contracts, they have pocketed their rack rents;   commerce and industry have tried to flourish on their soil, but time and time again, failure and loss have overtaken the tenants and the enterprising business man, but, as Mr. Johnston truly says— "The Campbells never failed; they sat still." They waited, knowing that the eternal years of God were theirs for exploitation.

It is an old problem in political ethics whether time brings forth Justice as a fruit of injustice. Some of these things happened three or four centuries ago; some of them happened half-a-century ago; many of them are still happening ! How far has the country as a whole acquiesced in the actions of these favoured individuals, and how far has its acquiescence bound their iniquities like a millstone round its neck ? Or, again, how far must the future be maimed by the folly of the past ? The forewords to a book such as this do not give an opportunity of a full discussion of these questions, but they do allow me to say, and to say most emphatically, that for the Roseberys, the Campbells, the Sutherlands, the Duffs, and the rest of "Our Scots Noble Families" who have grown rich by laying their hands upon property that belonged to other people and who have increased their estates by a ruthless exploitation of smallholders and peasant owners—for such men to speak of land taxation, compulsory land purchase, and the other items of a Socialist land programme as injustice, is nothing but impertinence and hypocrisy, which ought to be characterised as such in the plainest of language, both inside and outside of the House of Commons.

We are not on the defensive; we have no call to apologise. We are on the offensive, taking back from men who stole, withdrawing from classes that expropriated, the wealth that originally belonged to the community, that has been made valuable by the community, and that must, if ever social justice is to reign, be enjoyed by the community.

The restitution is to be difficult, I know. The law of conservation of energy holds good in Society as in Nature, and in the former it has some curious corollaries. One of them is that when an evil is done which is profitable to a section, even if it be a loss to the mass, it gathers round it interests which depend upon its continuation. Sometimes the interests are enjoyed by a few people. More commonly, however, a part of them is split up, and becomes enjoyed by many, whilst the possession of the great bulk is still retained by a small class. That is the case with land. Hundreds of little men, who have scraped together a few pounds, have invested them in a square yard or so of land. Friendly Societies have invested their funds in land. Trade Unions have put their accumulations in land. And the little man who can claim possession in soil not much broader or longer than is necessary for his grave, is willing to rise in arms to defend the wholesale exploitations of the Campbells of Blythswood, and the Sutherlands of Sutherlandshire. The appropriation of provinces is condoned because a £5 note has been invested in a plot.

The first step that has to be taken is to secure a proper valuation of all lands; to compile, in other words, a 20th Century Doomsday Book. This valuation must then be made the basis of taxation and rating, for it must be remembered that the Socialist has never committed himself to the position that the unearned increment in land is exclusively a local creation. When these steps are taken, we will be in a position to consider another method of dealing with the matter, viz., the method of purchase by national or local public authorities; and in the policy of purchase, compulsory powers will have to be made much more effective than they are now. More use can also be made of death duties, but these can rest for the moment where they are, whilst we are making a beginning with valuation and taxation. The compulsory production of titles would also be an interesting contribution to popular information regarding the honesty of the landed classes. The legal dictum of prescription would prevent a failure to produce titles being regarded as a proof that the owner had no legal titles to his land at all, but the educational value of such a thing would be great, and its influence in putting landed interests in a proper light in the eyes of public opinion would be incalculable.

Before concluding this introduction, I may be permitted to say that I welcome this book not merely for political, but also for historical reasons. There is a side of Socialism which appeals to the emotions, and which consists in clever criticism and descriptions of a literary character. But important as that is, it is not the propaganda that is to convert the country finally to our views. The scientific side of Socialism must be amplified, and I regard this book as a valuable contribution to that. The author's labours can be gauged by the wealth of his references, and much more of this work requires to be done. Have we, for instance, ever had a true history of the Reformation in Scotland ? We have had a gaily-coloured pageantry of battle and execution, of political and ecclesiastical turmoil, but I know of no history of Scotland which traces any re-adjustment of economic and political power as the meaning and the result of this wonderful time. The history of the people of Scotland yet remains to be written. The more impartially this is done, the more invaluable will it be as a propagandist manual. The story of the people in history is the best handbook for the guidance of the people in politics. It will not be pleasant reading altogether—except to the man of great faith, who sees in the past a record of the progress of imperfect, irrational, sinful man, plodding through mistakes and ignorance, ingratitude and treason, a weary and hard way up towards more happiness and greater perfection.

J. Ramsay MacDonald.

A GENERAL INDICTMENT.

BEFORE PROCEEDING to analyse the methods by which each of our Scots noble families rose to fortune, and before I examine in detail the origin of their various divinities, dignities, and privileges, it is advisable to take our canvas and lay on in primary colours a general and comprehensive indictment of Scots landlords as a class. The histories of our land have been mostly written to serve the political purposes, and flatter the conceits of our aristocracy. When the historian knew of happenings calculated to cast odium on our landed gentry, he carefully excised the records, and where he did not know, he was careful to assume, and lead others to assume, that the periods of which he was ignorant were periods of intense social happiness, wherein a glad and thankful populace spent their days and their nights in devising Hallelujahs in honour of the neighbouring nobleman. And that is why the history of Scots mining is wrapped in darkness: that is why we never hear of the hundred and fifty years slavery, and why the collier of to-day does not know that his ancestor of a century ago was a two-legged chattel, bought, sold, and lashed as were the cotton plantation negroes in pre-Civil War times. There are no popular histories of the thefts of the Klaan and Abbey lands. Even the sparse records of neyfship are never dragged out to the popular gaze. A democracy ignorant of the past is not qualified either to analyse the present or to shape the future; and so, in the interests of the High Priests of Politics and the Lordly Money-Changers of Society, great care has been taken to offer us stories of useless pageantry, chronicles of the birth and death of Kings, annals of Court intrigue and international war, while withheld from us were the real facts and narratives of moment, the loss of our ancient freedom, the rape of our common lands and the shameless and dastardly methods by which a few selected stocks snatched the patrimony of the people.

Generation after generation, these few families of tax-gatherers, have sucked the life-blood of our nation; in their prides and lusts they have sent us to war, family against family, clan against clan, race against race; that they might live in idleness and luxury, the labouring man has sweated and starved; they have pruned the creeds of our Church and stolen its revenues; their mailed fists have crushed the newer thought, and their vanities the arts. In their vandalisms they burned and destroyed our national records.

To-day the stones of old Kilwinning Abbey erect stabling at Eglinton Castle; Greyfriars Monastery went to erect Lord Maxwell's castle; Arbroath and Newbottle were despoiled for the erection of jails; the stones of Loretto built a Tolbooth; Melrose built a jail, a mansion house, and a mill; and Sweetheart Abbey went to rear a village.

Our very history has been inverted to fan their conceits; they have barred us by barbed wire fences from the bens and the glens: the peasant has been ruthlessly swept aside to make room for the pheasant, and the mountain hare now breeds her young on the hearthstone of the Gael! Time and again they have sold our land to the invader. The Bruce, a Norman, convinced our forefathers that his fight against the English was for Scottish freedom; and, lo, when the invading hosts were driven back, the Bruce handed our common fields to his fellow Normans. For the Stuarts, also Normans, we shed our blood, only to find the chains of tyranny and misery manacle us the more.

Professor Cowan, of Aberdeen, told us in 1901 that in the age before the Reformation "one-half of Scottish wealth was in ecclesiastical hands." At and after the Reformation we found the nobles who had allied themselves to our cause, not only foisting a hateful patronage upon our pulpits, but burning the ancient charters, grabbing the lands, and despoiling the patrimony of the kirk.

A General Indictment.

They scorned every principle of morality we hold dear; they gambled and murdered and robbed and foisted numerous children of illegitimate lusts on the granaries of the common people. For almost two centuries (see Appendix) they actually enslaved the miners of Scotland, buying and selling them like cattle, and lashing them to a miserable toil. In the Highlands, and on the Lowland Borders, they stole the clan lands and drove our kinsmen beyond the seas; they destroyed our ancient freedom, corrupted our laws, despoiled us of our common heritage, the soil, and to-day take rents for which they cannot produce titles. They are mostly—I am safe in saying 75 per cent of them—descendants of foreign freebooters, who forcibly took possession of our land after the Norman conquest in 1066. Year after year they still drive the people from the soil, huddling them in stinking cities, bereft of opportunities for the only trade they know, agriculture. And so the poor's rate rises and competition among city labourers for vacant situations becomes keener and wages fall. And so misery and drunkenness and destitution and physical degeneration eat like evil ghouls at the very fibre of our national life. And all because, forsooth, His Grace of Sutherland gets bigger rents for sheep farms than for crofts, and because His Grace of Atholl must have freedom on his August moors and solitude in his embattled keep. In the six crofting counties alone, in the 25 years from 1883 to 1908, deer forest lands increased by 1,248,598 acres, while in the non-crofting counties the lands exclusively devoted to sport in the year 1908 amounted to 563,688 acres. At the census of 1891 there were recorded 928,513 persons in the rural districts; at the census of 1901 there were only 885,809, or a decrease of 42,704 in 10 years. These figures tell the story of the strangulation of a race; they tell us that the Celt is being slowly, if silently, cleared from the croft of his fathers, and that soon no sound will echo in the smiling valleys but the crack of the sportsman's rifle and the plaintive cry of the lonely whaup. So long as a dozen families own one-half of Scotland, so long will countless families own none of it, and be under continual necessity of cringing before and begging:–

"A brother of the earth to give him leave to toil!"

And so long as half the race is compelled by dire necessity to kneel cap-in-hand before the Lord who "owns" the soil, so long will our rural populations be cast in an unmanly and spiritless mould. This, indeed, I take to be fundamentally the most serious evil wrought by private landlordism in Scotland to-day. To extort rents, to enclose fields, to drive the peasant from his croft that the pheasant may be plentiful and "free from disease" (which solicitude about health is by no means so frequently extended to the children of the farm labourer), to withhold land required for public improvements, or to give it only at ransom prices and with iniquitous reservations, to shut out the people from the beauties of the sylvan glade, to fence them out with Trespass Boards and barbed wire from the mountain peak or the moor or the loch, to herd them in smoky cities—these are grievous wrongs. But to sit as feudal superiors dictating to men and women how they shall comport themselves alike in the great and the trivial affairs of life, to prohibit marriages, by refusing house accommodation, to crush and grind the soul, the manliness, the backbone, and the independence out of rural Scotland, to have every man, woman, and child cap-touching, curtseying, fetching, and carrying, and currying favour, is to perpetrate a crime far more terrible than is bodily hurt or theft of gear. To-day the shadow of the "Big House" blights and withers the soul of the villager; he votes, thinks, and prays (or pretends to), as factor and flunkey suggest; his initiative, his individuality, his spirit has been crushed.

Wilde, in that brilliant essay of his on "The Soul of Man," declared that the, to him, sad thing about the French Revolution was not that Marie Antoinette went to the scaffold, but that there could be found peasants in La Vendee willing to go to death for the hideous cause of Feudalism. And to-day, in Scotland, our artisans and peasants appear to believe that these ancient noble families hold their privileges and lands at the earnest behest of Divine Providence; that their wealth has been justly earned; and that their titles are but rewards for honest service to the State.

A General Indictment.

The first step in Reform, either of the Land Laws or of the House of Lords, is to destroy these superstitions. Show the people that our Old Nobility is not noble, that its lands are stolen lands—stolen either by force or fraud; show people that the title-deeds are rapine, murder, massacre, cheating, or Court harlotry; dissolve the halo of divinity that surrounds the hereditary title; let the people clearly understand that our present House of Lords is composed largely of descendants of successful pirates and rogues; do these things and you shatter the Romance that keeps the nation numb and spellbound while privilege picks its pockets. The following papers (most of which have appeared in the columns of *Forward*) have an enormous research work embodied in them, and are now gathered together at the earnest request of a large number of people who believe it to be necessary that the information should not be left buried in a newspaper file, but should be widely disseminated among all varieties of Social Reformers. It is scarcely necessary to add that these papers pretend to be no more than mere preliminary indictments, affording, perhaps, a basis on which future democratic historians will build, but in themselves merely stray leaves from the records of the past, hastily linked together to form a suitable weapon for the campaigns of the immediate future.

OUR SCOTS
NOBLE FAMILIES

THE GORDONS OF BARRA:

AND THE VATERSAY SQUATTINGS.

"For the information of our readers, we now give the manner in which the Barra crofters have been reduced to their present condition. When kelp was in great demand, the former proprietor started a kelp manufactory, at which the services of all the spare hands in the islands were required. He always preferred labour to money; and when he found that the crofters could pay their rent in three months, he increased his claims gradually until each crofter required to keep a labourer there all the year round. After the manufacturing of kelp stopped, the rents continued at the same figure. This is the whole secret of the Barra destitution." *Macleod's "Gloomy Memories."*

"I am a lover of law and order, but there are times when men could not stand it any longer. This land was occupied by their fore-fathers, and they had a better right to it than Lady Gordon Cathcart."
Mr. J. G. Weir, M.P. for Ross and Cromarty, in House of Commons, 25th June, 1908.

"There is no population in the world who so rapidly entwine themselves into your affections than the inhabitants of those bleak and desolate districts."
Right Hon. A. J. Balfour (same time and place).

"When the bold kindred in the time long-vanished,
Conquered the soil and fortified the keep;
No seer foretold the children would be banish'd,
That a degenerate lord might boast his sheep."
Professor Wilson.

I HAVE had great difficulty in tracing the lineage of this "noble" family. Burke's "Landed Gentry" knows them not under the names of either Gordon or Cathcart, but Mackenzie, in his "Short History of the Highlands," says that all the estates in the outer islands changed hands during the last century. And this may, somehow, be the reason why they are dropped from the "gentry" lists. The Landowners' Return, however, gives "John Gordon of Cluny Castle, South Uist," as the owner of 84,404 acres in Inverness-shire (rental, £8954), and as Cluny Castle is an ancient "seat" of the Huntly Gordons, we may start with the fair presumption that the kind-hearted Christian lady who lately had the ten men of Vatersay consigned to prison for squatting on a bleak and barren shore, scraping an unkindly earth for food for their children, and, withal, offering rent for the privilege—we may start, I say, with the presumption that she is, through marriage, a genuine Huntly Gordon of the real old tooth-and-talon breed.

She is a granddaughter of Sir John Pringle of Stichell, Dumfries-shire, and while still on the sunny side of 20 summers, married John Gordon of Cluny, son of the Colonel Gordon mentioned hereafter. In 1880, two years after Mr. Gordon's death, she married Sir Reginald Cathcart, of whom history relates little beyond the fact that he is a keen sportsman and visits the "island home" annually, "as it comprises one of the best salmon and sea trout fishings in the Highlands." He does not "trouble himself much with estate management," we are told; and as Lady Gordon Cathcart has not visited Barra for some 30 years, we assume that this noble pair are interested in Barra—chiefly at rent times.

The first "Barra" Gordon I can come across was a gallant Colonel who "owned" the islands about 58 years ago. He appears to have been one of the most inhuman rascals that even Scottish land history takes cognisance of, and after reading the history of the Barra evictions as given in an old issue of the Quebec *Times*, I feel that beside him Nero was an innocent babe, and Genseric a sort of early version of Sweet Saint Francis of Assisi.

In the summer of 1851 the "gallant" Colonel opined that the small croft system was not paying him enough rent, and he devised one of the most infernal schemes for getting rid of the crofters that a fiend could imagine. There was an extreme potato blight that year; the people were crying for food; distress was terrible; great public meetings of sympathy were held, and huge sums of money were raised to alleviate the distress; the poor's rate rose enormously; the Highland proprietors got up a clamour; Colonel Gordon vainly endeavoured to get rid of Barra altogether by offering to sell it to the State for penal settlement purposes. Then, when the crofters were getting desperate, the Government transferred the grant which had previously been given for the improvement and cultivation of the Highlands, to an emigration scheme fund. This was the Colonel's chance. If the people would not go, he would make them. He brought transport ships up to Loch Boisdale, and his agents commanded the miserable people to assemble at that place under a penalty of £2 for abstention. When there many of them were forcibly seized, and despite the most frantic entreaties, were carried aboard. Some who resisted were handcuffed. Others, who either refused to go to the meeting, or who had cleared off ere the pressgang got to work, were hunted and chased over the hills like wild beasts. One gentleman who chanced to be in Barra at the time, wrote:–

> "Were you to see the racing and chasing of policemen,
> constables, and ground officers pursuing the outlawed
> natives, you would think, only for their colour, that
> you had been by some miracle transported to the banks
> of the Gambia on the Slave Coast of Africa."

Frail old men were shipped off while more agile members of their families prowled around the remote glens and mountain tops of their native island. Families were ruthlessly broken up; fathers and mothers sent across the black ocean, their children torn from their sides to be sent by another emigrant ship; houses were razed to the ground. The Rev. Henry Beatson (local clergyman) appears to have been a despicable cur. It is said of him that during the slave hunt, he made "himself very officious, as he always does when he has an opportunity of oppressing the poor Barra men, and of gaining the favour of Colonel Gordon. In fact, he is the most vigilant and assiduous officer Colonel Gordon has. He may be seen in Castle Bay, the principal anchorage in Barra, whenever a sail is hoisted directing his men, like a gamekeeper with his hounds, in case any of the doomed Barramen should escape, so that he might get his land cultivated and improved for nothing. They offered one day to board an Arran boat who had a poor man concealed, but the master, John Crawford, lifted a hand-spike, and threatened to split the skull of the first man who would attempt to board his boat, and thus the poor Barraman escaped their clutches."*

In all, between 1500 and 2000 people were thus transported. Fancy the groaning and wailing from that huddled, starving, despairing mass on deck!

"We ne'er shall tread the fancy-haunted valley,
Where 'tween the dark hills creeps the small clear stream;
In arms around the patriarch banner rally,
Nor see the moon on royal tombstones gleam."

No, never again.

And hungered, hopeless women screaming in the Gaelic for the sons they would never see again; fathers peering through the mist for one long last look at the little shieling of the sacred memories; children crying aimlessly in sympathy with the general sorrow—all alike facing a six weeks' voyage, ill-fed, ill-clad, mid sickness, disease, and foul excrement; torn from their native land to be cast like human driftwood on an alien shore; knowing not the English language; with not a penny in their pockets, and with nothing but despair in their hearts. See them, a pitiful procession, their children on their backs, begging at the homesteads of a strange land, wandering famine-shrunken and helpless, on the outskirts of Toronto and Hamilton!

---

* Macleod's "Gloomy Memories of the Highlands"

Famine and cold decimate their ranks. See the mothers wrap the frozen remains of their dead infants in a few frozen rags and with the Celtic wail of despair consign them to a hole in the frozen earth!

Against the author of these crimes there seems to have been a strong feeling of indignation in Canada. The Quebec *Times*, after detailing the circumstances of the "immigration," said:–

> "The expulsion of these unfortunate creatures from their homes—the man-hunt with the policeman and bailiffs—the violent separation of families—the parents torn from the child, the mother from her daughter—the infamous trickery practised on those who did embark—the abandonment of the aged, the infirm women and tender children in a foreign land—form a tableau which cannot be dwelt on for an instant without horror. Words cannot depict the atrocity of the deed. For cruelty less savage, the dealers of the South have been held up to the execration of the world."

In that year, 1851, *every crofter in Barra was evicted, and everything they possessed was confiscated.*

That statement must seem almost incredible to the average Liberal or Tory who is only slowly being weaned away from his ancient political allegiance, but I make it on the authority of Mr. Dewar, Liberal Member of Parliament for South Edinburgh.

Before I briefly review the events that led up to the Vatersay squattings, let me insist on the undoubted fact that these outer islands are capable of great agricultural development, that they were once able to bear a well-fed peasantry, and that private landlordism and private landlord greed, short-sighted (as greed always is) and unscrupulous, has not only been the ruin of the peasantry but has been the ruin of their agriculture as well.

Sir Donald Munro, High Dean of the Isles, is quoted by Lord Colin Campbell in "The Crofter in History" as reporting in 1549 that Barra is "ane fertill and fruitfull ile in cornes."

"Nowhere," says his Lordship, "does the Dean lead us to infer that scarcity prevailed among these people. Nor, beyond some notices of the haunts of thieves and rebels, is there any hint that their condition was one of insecurity."

In Skene's "Celtic Scotland" we are told that about 1595 Barra supplied 200 fighting men, and must therefore have had a population of some 1200 people at least, because "na labourers of the ground are permittit to steer furth of the countrie quhatevir their master have ado."

Later on—in James the VI's time—we find that the Marquis of Huntly has undertaken "the extirpation of the barbarous people of the Isles within a year," in reward for which kindly piece of Statecraft he was to have "a feu of the North Isles, excepting Skye and Lewis."

About the beginning of the Eighteenth Century, one Martin, wrote of the Islands as being "fruitful in corn," and showed that the people of Barra caught salmon for their own use, being evidently troubled by no nonsense about "preserved" water. The local chieftain, "Mackneil of Barra," took a fatherly interest in the people, saw that none starved, provided suitable wives for widowers, and when any of his tenants "are so far advanced in years that they are incapable to till the ground, Mackneil takes such old men into his own family and maintains them all their life after."

But after the Rebellion of 1745, Pennant tells us that the price of cattle doubled, as did rents; agriculture was not encouraged; sheep walks and large farms gradually crushed the peasantry to the sea-shore, and although Dr. Walker reported to the Commissioners the immediate necessity of the reversal of that policy, and the dissemination of the latest information as to agricultural advance, his advice was unheeded, and the sheep continued to destroy the corn land.

Then in 1851 came the scandalous evictions and forced emigration already detailed.

Now for the history of the last twenty-five years! After the clearance of 1851, there was, as was natural, tranquility for a time; but the island population gradually increased, and 25 years ago the sea-shore *miserables* living precariously on whelks and offal, fiercely began to demand land to live upon. They offered a fair rent. They declared that their decayed huts were reeking with typhus, typhoid, and scarlet fever.* Time after time they petitioned the proprietrix for land, and on most occasions were not even given the courtesy of a reply. The local Parish Council humbly petitioned her on behalf of the people, but got never a reply. Latterly the Inverness County Council—Tory almost to a man—stepped in and sent a deputation to Barra and Vatersay. The deputation held a nine days' enquiry, and reported:–

> "Land was available, urgently required, would be highly beneficial, and could not be obtained by the Parish Council on reasonable terms."

Latterly in 1906, the people, driven to desperation, swarmed over to the Island of Vatersay, and began small crofts there, offering rent, which was refused by the proprietrix. Then all over the country a great landlord hullaballoo was raised. The Court of Session ordered the squatters to clear off Vatersay and go back to their Barra hovels and shellfish. It was not the mere matter of 10 poor men on a semi-barren rock in the Atlantic; it was the whole principle of landlordism that was at stake. The leader of the Tory opposition (Mr. Balfour) was produced in Glasgow while the case was still *sub judice* to howl about the landlords' rights, and the *Scotsman* (Tory newspaper) knowing that there was no contempt of court when the question was between 10 poor islanders and the whole landlord

---

* Of the ten men imprisoned for squatting on Vatersay, every one has had fever in his house, and seven of the ten have lost relatives through these fevers.

class of the country, broke in on 29th January, while the case was still before the Court, with:–

> "Her (Lady Gordon Cathcart's) fault has been habitual and perhaps unwise indulgence of the cotters, who are now repaying her generous and considerate policy by forcible seizure and wanton injury."

The squatters, of course, could not obey the Court of Session's injunction, and they were thereupon summoned for contempt of Court; and as they had no money with which to travel to Edinburgh, Lady Gordon Cathcart, as the Tory press puts it, "kindly offered to pay their rail fare" —an offer I regret to say the squatters were induced to accept. On landing in Edinburgh, they were promptly given two months' imprisonment.

The Landowners' Return already quoted gives the annual rental of the lands owned by the Gordon Family in Inverness-shire as £8954, a sum which immediately forces us to the conclusion that Lady Gordon Cathcart does not eat whelks.

In the year 1883 the proprietrix let out a portion of the Barra lands for small crofts, but when in 1888 the Crofters' Commission visited these same small crofts, they found she was charging exorbitant rents, so exorbitant that they were promptly reduced by 35 per cent. For the few acres she sold to the Congested Districts Board she got £7500, or $38\frac{1}{2}$ years' purchase; and when the land in question was properly valued by the Commissioners, it was found to be worth only £5500—a clear overcharge of £2000. Sixty acres she had let in Vatersay for 2/- an acre, she managed to sell at £600, equal to 100 years' purchase!

Water in Barra is brought from a lake through pipes three-quarters of a mile long, and for this each fisherman is charged 10/ per season, which means £200 a year to the proprietrix. Despite all this, we are told the people live in houses that are

> "like enlarged bee-hives, mere temporary erections, closely packed together, and built in a bog."

Is it much wonder that "this estate is perpetually in trouble "; is it much wonder that the Government has required to interfere three times since 1883; is it much wonder that the people are determined to stand no further nonsense from this predatory nest of Gordons, and that they decline any longer to live on dulse and whelks while an idle landlord, who seems ashamed to show her face in Barra, struts abroad with a yearly income of almost £9000, practically all of it wrung from the misery and degradation of the poor islanders?

THE PRIMROSES.

"We find the inhabitants of this earth broadly divided into two great masses; the peasant paymasters—spade in hand, original and imperial producers of turnips; and, waiting on them all round, a crowd of polite persons, modestly expectant of turnips, for some—too often theoretical—service."   *Ruskin.*

"Do you imagine that these poor men can avoid think-ing, that it is through their own cowardice that such incapable people are wealthy, or that they can refrain from repeating to one another, when they meet in private—'Our governors are naught?' "
Plato: "Republic," Book VIII.

"Morality and Political Economy unite in repelling the individual who consumes without producing."
De Balzac.

THE PRIMROSES, the family to which the Earl of Rosebery belongs, have only sprung up in comparatively recent times; and consequently they have not had many opportunities of perpetrating land robberies or of steeping themselves in deceit, cruelty, and blood. At the time of the last Landowners' Return, Lord Rosebery owned in Scotland, lands as follows:–

Edinburgh County—	*Acres.*	*Gross Annual Rental.*
Earl of Rosebery	15,568	8,973
Earl of Rosebery (Mines)	—	200
Linlithgowshire—		
Earl of Rosebery	5,680	8,902
Earl of Rosebery (Mines)	—	2,416
	21,248	£20,491

Since that time he has added considerably to his acreage. He is now the possessor of 7000 acres in Linlithgow and 18,500 acres in Midlothian; he also owns some 5500 acres in Buckingham, 2000 in Norfolk, 5300 in Herts, 170 in Kent, and 3 in Suffolk. So that although he killed the Scots Small Holdings Bill, he himself has taken care to see that he has room to plant a few cabbages.

Little is known of the origin of the family; but according to Burke's "Peerage," the earliest traceable ancestor was one Duncan Primrose, who had sprung from the lands of Primrose in County Fife, and who "was seated at Culross in Perthshire in the reign of Queen Mary, and who married Janet, daughter of Main, of Arthur House." From this marriage arose a generation or two of theologians, who appear to have been engaged in the conversion of the "papishry" of France, and in writing sundry luminous works on the "Sabbath and the Lord's Day," and kindred subjects. One of them had got himself utterly detested by the French and was obliged to quit the country. But it is from another son of Duncan Primrose that Lord Rosebery is descended.

Archibald Primrose was employed as a scrivener or clerk by the Abbot of Culross; and he appears to have been engaged in fixing the rates of feu-duties to be paid by the vassals of the Abbey. His son, James, became a lawyer and was raised by King James to the post of Clerk of the Privy Council. This gentleman married twice, and had nineteen children, one of whom married the Court jeweller, Heriot (of Heriot Trust fame), and another of whom, Archibald, became a baronet, and, ultimately, Lord Carrington. These titles he received from King Charles II for his services to the Royalist cause, and for his labours as Clerk to the Privy Council (in which position he had succeeded his father) and as Clerk to the Convention of Estates. He was a consistently anti-Parliament man, but when after the Restoration he discovered that the Merry Monarch had granted Sir William Fleming the post of Lord-Clerk Register, his faith in royalty must have been sorely tried; still he seems to have had some ready cash, for he managed to buy off Sir William, and to obtain the sinecure for himself. This Cavalier was the real founder of the family fortunes, and if Bishop Burnet's estimate of Primrose's character is to be accepted—and the Bishop knew Primrose intimately—then Lord Rosebery has not inherited his estates from Sir Archibald Primrose, but his subtilty and selfishness as well. How is this for a character sketch of Lord Rosebery?

> * "The subtilest of all Lord Midletoun's friends was Sir Archibald Primerose. . . He was a dexterous man in business: he had always expedients ready at every difficulty. He had an art of speaking to all men according to their sense of things; and so drew out their secrets, while he concealed his own; for words went for nothing with him. He said everything that was necessary to persuade those he spoke to, that he was of their mind; and did it in so genuine a way, that he seemed to speak his heart. He was always for soft counsels and slow methods; and thought that the chief thing that a great man ought to do was to raise his family and his kindred, who naturally stick to him; for he had seen so much of the world that he did not depend much on friends, and so took no care in making any. He always advised the Earl of Midletoun to go slowly in the King's business; but to do his own effectually, before the King should see he had no further occasion for him."

Isn't there something almost uncanny about that limning of Lord Rosebery some 300 years before he was born? Looking after Number One, persuasive, dexterous, words meaning little to him; a *soupçon* of the cynic about him; ploughing the lonely furrow. Hear further of this ancestor of the Apostle of Thrift:–

> † "Primrose was grown rich and cautious; and his own maxim had always been, that, when he apprehended a change, he ought to lay in for it by courting the side that was depressed, that so in the next turn he might secure friends to himself, he began to think that the Earl of Midletoun went too fast to hold out long."

* "The History of My Own Times" by Bishop Burnet. Vol. I., p.179.
† Ibid. P. 250

So Primrose had grown both rich and cautious. Mr. Coates in his "History of Lord Rosebery," says that Primrose purchased the lands of Primrose from the Earl of Haddington; but this soft-spoken, underhand, Sir Archibald, lived in times when there were many curious methods of "purchasing" estates. We know that Primrose was a "great dealer" in accepting "presents" from such of the Gentry as did not wish to be interfered with on account of their religion §; and we know that when the King sent down the Earl of Nithsdale to demand that the Scots Nobles who had stolen the lands belonging to the Church should immediately hand them over to the Crown, these pirates "most concerned" met in Edinburgh and agreed "if no other argument did prevail to make the Earl of Nithsdale desist, they would fall upon him and all his party in the old Scottish manner and knock them on the head." ¶

Old Lord "Belhaven of the name of Douglas, who was blind, bid them set him by one of the party, and he would make sure of one." King James VI of Scotland was perhaps about the best of the Stuarts, and seems to have been an honest and comparatively humane sort of man at heart; but he was no match for the noble Scots vultures of his day, and Nithsdale was glad to scurry back with his skin whole.

Considering then the gang that Primrose was hand in glove with, and considering the character of the man himself, it will take more that Mr. Coates' bare *ipse dixit* to convince the student of Scots land history that Primrose paid honest money for the lands now held by the Rosebery family.

Observe then the founder of the "thrifty" family! A traitor to his friends, ready to sell them as occasion arose; a sneak; an accepter of presents, venal to such a degree that even in a venal age, the historian singles him out for remark. When the rats were deserting Lord Middletoun's sinking ship, Primrose was one of the first to leave.

§ Ibid. P. 194.
¶ Ibid. P. 35.

He got clear in time, and managed to retain his offices. But in 1678 he was removed to less well-paid posts. His son and successor by dint of great ability raised himself to the onerous and responsible position of gentleman of the bedchamber to Prince George of Denmark. He succeeded also in marrying an English heiress and getting himself created Earl of Rosebery, Viscount of Inverkeithing, and Lord Dalmeny and Primrose. They have as a general rule married well, these Roseberys, and have contracted alliances with, among other families, the Argylls and the Lothians. But the present Earl, in marrying the heiress of the Rothschilds, Hannah, has gone one better. Lord Rosebery, of course, has done good work on the London County Council—work which it would be foolish and churlish to mitigate or deny. He has however travelled backwards since then; he, the millionaire by marriage, he who spends thousands annually on sport, now lectures the working classes on "Thrift." His son and heir, Lord Dalmeny, M.P. for Midlothian—M.P. until such time as the workers there waken up politically, appears to be a bright specimen of the young nobility, if we may judge from the sporting pages of the Glasgow *Herald* of 3rd April, 1908:–

LORD DALMENY THE OBJECT OF A HOSTILE DEMONSTRATION

A regrettable incident occurred at the Vale of Aylesbury Steeplechases yesterday. Only two horses went to the post for the Heavy-Weight Steeplechase, these being Lord Dalmeny's Kilcullen II. And Lord Gort's Git the Coin, both ridden by their owners. On passing the stands the first time round Lord Dalmeny was leading, but shortly afterwards his horse dropped behind, and although Git the Coin fell, it was remounted, and assuming the lead, won easily. Lord Dalmeny thereupon met with a hostile demonstration from the occupants of the grand stand and others, and there was considerable booing. Lord Dalmeny is stated to have accounted for the occurrence by the fact that during the first mile and a half of the race his horse ran away with him, and was consequently unable to re-spond to his call in the latter part of the race.

Comment on this would be improper.

THE CAMPBELLS OF BLYTHSWOOD

AND THE COMMON LANDS OF GLASGOW.

"Thou shalt not steal."   —*The Bible.*

THE late Sir James Marwick, Town Clerk of Glasgow, in his "Charters and Documents relating to the City," shows a map of the old regality of Glasgow. This map includes the land now enclosed by a circle with its line laid through Scotstoun, Jordanhill, Cadder, Muckroft (north of Chryston), to the east of Bedlay, almost at Airdrie, Woodhall, back to the Cadder Water to the north of Rutherglen, south by Strathbungo and by South Govan back to Scotstoun again. All this was once the common land of Glasgow. In still earlier days the Bishops of Glasgow held, from the Crown, and for behoof of the people, an even larger territory, but it was gradually encroached upon by the marauding barons and land pillagers, until it dwindled down to a mere fraction of its former size. When the land was held by the Church, many communal enterprises were undertaken, and we have indication that coal-mines* and lime-stone quarries, corn mills, farming, etc., were all worked for the common good. Then came the Reformation and the Church lands eventually—for the most part at least—handed over to the Provost and Magistrates of the City of Glasgow—handed over of course during the pleasure of the Crown and for the benefit of the citizens. No historian has yet

---

* The City owned 12 coalpits (see M'Ure's History, p. 121-2), and in 1649, when the Town Council agreed to set "a coal and lyme craig on lease, they reserved the liberty to work it themselves" (Renwick, "Glasgow Memorials," p. 132).

searched the musty files and fly-blown documents to give us a careful and exact history of how these common lands of ours disappeared into the capacious maw of private property. Those who could speak—well, it is not their business, and as we have no land agitations in our Council Chamber except the sporadic and watery Taxing of Land Values debates, and as no Councillor has as yet managed to force the necessary data from our Town Clerks, we are still practically in the dark as to the nefarious practices by which we lost our Common Lands.

Unlike some of the "Noble" families whose histories we are now considering, the Campbells of Blythswood do not appear to have founded their affluence on murder, rapine, or flagrant and open theft. The Campbell of Blythswood origin is rather *bourgeois*; they were of the merchant princes and swaggered it in the Trongate with their silk stockings and snuff-boxes. Away as far back as the Reign of Queen Mary, when the City of Glasgow could only boast 4500 inhabitants, the Campbells were traders, and had a comfortable old mansion house in the Bridgegate. A Colin Campbell was Provost in 1615; his only son, also called Colin, was Provost in 1639. The second son of the latter, again a Colin, was Provost in 1661; and his brother James was Provost in 1669. The Colin who was Provost in 1639 seems to have been a shrewd gentleman in all that pertains to land speculation; for, when Sir George Elphinstone, the owner of the Blythswood estate, died in 1634, so poor that his very body was arrested by his creditors, Colin Campbell purchased the estate from the unhappy pawnbrokers, and although I cannot discover the price paid, we can assume that the holders would be only too glad to realise something, no matter how small, and that they would part with Blythswood to the Provost, at a price convenient and profitable to the latter gentleman.

At anyrate, this same Provost Colin managed to wheedle the Town Council into giving him 1,892,150 square yards of the Common Land—that part on which the west of the city now lies— for what is described as a "wanworth." A wanworth of that period was sometimes defined as "the feeding of ane hen for ane year," and was really regarded as a sort of courtesy payment. As an illustration of this let us take the "wanworth" paid by Sir James Turner for the Gorbals houses and lands. This Gorbals transaction took place in the same Council as "wanworthed" away the western lands to Provost Colin Campbell. Here is the Turner swindle verbatim from the Corporation Records of date 18th July, 1670:–

> "The Baillies and Counsel 'ordains ane tack to be wrytten and subscryvit in favours of Sir James Turnor of the tounnes houss and tour in Gorbals, quhilk he presentlie possesses, and that dureing his lyfetyme, for payments yearlie of thrie punds Scots (5/), gif the samyne be requyred.' "

Gif the samyne be required!

Now, if the Council were so generous with the property of the people when the recipient was a mere outsider like Sir James Turner, what extravagances of liberality would they not display when the happy recipient was the Provost?

Here are almost two million yards of valuable land swallowed up by the Campbells of Blythswood. No one knows what they paid for it, no one knows if they paid anything for it. The late Mr. Henry George, at a meeting in the City Hall, Glasgow, on 18th February, 1884, stated that he "had been informed" that the Provost had given £1500 for the gold-mine. But who was his informant? Where did he get the information? The present-day taxers of land values have no information on the subject. But suppose the Provost *did* pay £1500 for the land, that sum only figures out AT HALF-A-FARTHING PER SQUARE YARD, and the Editor of the *Glasgow Herald*, writing in 1850, was surely justified in commenting thus:–

> "Whatever blame there may be in this Blythswood annexation transaction, would lie fully as much with the Council for giving, as with Mr. Campbell for accepting."

Just so. But do you wonder that the Lords of Blythswood are "consistently Conservative, and subscribe largely to all properly-managed funds for the obstruction of predatory schemes of taxing land, etc.?"

At anyrate, there's where your land has gone, ye citizens of Glasgow. The feu-duties taken on this land I have seen variously stated at sums ranging from £30,000 to £45,000 per annum; but these figures I expect are largely guesswork; there is no reliable data to go upon in the Landowners' Return of 1874, the Campbell estates being unaccountably omitted from its pages.

The St. Vincent Street United Free Church pays, I am told, Two Pounds per week to Lord Blythswood for the privilege of erecting a chapel in which to worship God. Two pounds must be popped into the plate every Sabbath ere the citizens are free to worship; and that £2 is promptly scooped up by the descendant of a man who, in virtue of his Provostship, secured nearly two million acres of the people's land—without their consent, of course—for a mere "wanworth."

Some of these "defenders of the faith" are interesting gentry, when we begin to analyse their bank accounts.

In the Town Council's minutes for 16th September, 1704, we find the same successful sneaking behind bargains and getting the better of the people of Glasgow. Five roods or thereby of the "toune's common" had been enclosed (that is, stolen), by Campbell of Woodside. There had somehow or other been an outcry and investigation, and the Campbells had been asked to pay £60 for the land. But on September 16th there appears a minute graciously waiving away the claim to the £60, on the somewhat vague and uncertain ground that Colin Campbell "hes been att expensses and trouble of late in severall affairs of this burgh."

Still the humour of the proceeding does not end there, and by another minute of 1st October, 1709, it appears that the Campbells had been due "two hundred and twenty punds" debt on the land in question, and then follows the curious recommend-ation, which I suppose was unanimously passed, that, as in addition to the "expenses and trouble" argument already mentioned, there were "other weighty considerationes" why the Campbells should be freed from this debt "for now and ever," the claim on the Campbell land encroachers should be entirely dropped.

Up till the year 1804 the rents drawn by the Campbells from this annexed land were comparatively small, but in that year, one William Harley, a merchant, took a large feu, and erected in Bath Street large dairies, baths, and other buildings. Poor Harley, however, could not hold on long enough: he spent too much, and he failed. Succeeding speculators, Mr. Archibald Cuthel, writer, Mr. James Cooke, engineer, and others, also failed; but the Campbells never failed. They sat still; even as they slept the city was extending westwards, prices of land rose, feu-duties and ground annuals went up, and the Campbells pocketted the increase, waxed fat, became aristocratic, entertained Royalty, opposed reform—all from the rents drawn from the land that should to-day belong to the City of Glasgow.

Yet even if we grant that the "deal" by which they got the lands was legal, all their other transactions in the amassing of wealth can hardly bear the light of day. Take the case of poor Lin Dillon, the English plasterer, and how he was robbed.

I cull the following particulars from an article by "Senex." in the *Glasgow Herald*, of 1850. "Senex" declared that he took the facts from the printed papers that were laid before the Court of Session:–

> "On the 22nd of May, 1770, James Campbell of Blythswood granted a Tack to Lin Dillon, a plasterer, and to his heirs or assignees, of part of his garden, lying behind his mansion-house in the Bridgegate of Glasgow, for the space of 19 years, with breaks at the end of 7 and 13 years, 'and with liberty to erect shades (sheds) or other buildings thereupon; and the land-lord at the end of this Tack, to pay the value of the

said shades and buildings, as the same shall be ascertained by two persons, to be mutually chosen by the parties.'

"Mr. Jas. Campbell in the said Tack designed himself 'Heritable Proprietor of the Yard after mentioned.' Mr. Dillon then raised the ground of the garden about three feet, to prevent its being inundated during the ordinary floods of the river; built a dwelling-house of three floors upon it; also erected sheds, offices, and workhouses, and enclosed the ground with a brick wall; all these he did under the eye of Mr. James Campbell, who every day saw the buildings going on, and who expressed his approbation and satisfaction at the improvements making on the subjects. Dillon regularly paid the rent of the premises to Mr. James Campbell during his lifetime, as the same fell due.

"James Campbell of Blythswood died in the latter end of 1773, leaving no real personal estate whatever, after sick-bed and funeral charges were defrayed. His eldest son, John (afterwards Colonel Campbell), succeeded to the Blythswood entailed estates, to whom Dillon regularly paid the rent of the subjects, in conformity with the terms of his Tack. But, having entered into another line of business, he gave intimation to Colonel Campbell's factor, on the 2nd July, 1776, that he was going to quit the subjects, and give up the Tack, at the 'break' of seven years, viz., at Whitsunday, 1777; and again (no answer being returned) did the same in proper legal form at the term, when the first seven years of the Tack had expired, requesting a proper person to be named in order to ascertain the value of the buildings, so that the amount thereof might be paid to him, as provided by the Tack. This request being unattended to, or refused, Dillon brought an action against Colonel Campbell upon the Tack and circumstances before mentioned, and denying the validity of the Blythswood entail, in so far as regarded Burgage Tenements, concluding against Colonel Campbell, the defender, for £300, as the value of the buildings erected on the

Blythswood grounds under the faith of the Tack.

"When the case came before Lord Braxfield, Ordinary, Colonel Campbell appeared and pleaded as follows:– 'That he was heir of entail to the deceased James Campbell of Blythswood, and that as he represented him in that character only, so he could not be liable to the pursuer's claims.'

"The Lord Ordinary (8th December, 1778), took up Colonel Campbell's view of the case, assoilzied him from the action; reserving to Dillon his power to make his claim effectual against the other representatives of the last Blythswood, but this reservation was of no value to poor Dillon, as Mr. James Campbell had not left one farthing of available property.

"Dillon had one of the ablest advocates of the day for his counsel, viz., Robert Cullen, afterwards Lord Cullen, and he presented one of the most eloquent and most powerful memorials to the Court of Session that ever appeared there. The following is part of it, and the italics are in the original.

"'Mr. Campbell, who contracted with the pursuer, is now dead, and is succeeded by his son in a very opulent estate of more than £2000 sterling a year; but when this poor plasterer comes and says to him—*Perform your father's contract, and give me what the subjects are worth*, the defender tells him—*I am an heir of entail; I am not bound to fulfil any of my father's engagements; I will take and pocket your rents, and I will keep your buildings; but I won't pay you a single farthing*. And he adds this notable reason—*That he has prodigious occasion for money to buy himself up in the army*. Such is precisely the defence here maintained by this gentleman, who gets by his father so very large a fortune; and it just comes to this, that he will deprive this poor stranger of his whole fortune, and convert it to his own use, without giving him a penny of equivalent.' "

Until one makes a detailed investigation of the history of some of these "noble" families of ours, it is almost impossible to credit the mean and petty rascality on which they grew to affluence and plenty. Let me give another instance of that from the History of the Blythswoods. Mr. Tweed, in his "Glasgow: Ancient and Modern," declares that about 100 years ago there was a Glasgow baker who had an account against the Blythswoods for over £100. The chief of the Blythswood family—in whose name the goods had been ordered—died. In vain the baker rendered his account to the heir and to the other members of the family. In vain he "alleged that Colonel John, his two brothers, and five sisters, have all intromitted, art and part, in the act of consuming his bread." In vain the poor baker's account was repudiated—and the baker died. And here is the final touch:

> "It was thought, however, that Major Archibald, on succeeding to the Blythswood Estates, would have discharged the debt if he had been applied to in a gently and courteous manner, but that he considered the demand had been made upon him in a bullying and threatening style, which he was resolved to resist."

Noblesse oblige!

THE STAIRS.

"It is noteworthy that the nobles of the country (Scotland) have maintained a quite despicable behaviour from the days of Wallace downwards—a selfish, ferocious, famishing, unprincipled set of hyenas, from whom at no time, and in no way, has the country derived any benefit whatever."   *Carlyle.*

"Ravenous wolves who have enough and to spare, yet so greedy and covetous they will not suffer the poor to live in peace."   *Henryson.*

AT THE TIME of the last Landowners' Return, 1874, the Dalrymple Family (which began its "success" with a father who as Judge was known as "a great perverter of Justice" and a son who contrived and planned the massacre of Glencoe) had managed to amass unto itself the following spoil from Scotland:–

	Acres.	Gross Annual Rental.
Wigtownshire—		
Earl of Stair	79,174	£40,425
Trustees of the late Earl of Stair	3,492	3,084
Haddingtonshire—		
Earl of Stair	88	110
Charles Dalrymple of Hailes	1,698	4,586
Sir Hew Dalrymple of N. Berwick	3,039	8,856
Edinburgh—		
Trustees of the 8th Earl of Stair	8,384	4,988
Trustees of the 8th Earl of Stair (Mines)	—	270
Earl of Stair	4,118	3,165
Earl of Stair and Trustees of 8th Earl of Stair	1,325	2,359

Charles Dalrymple of Hailes	175	693
Buteshire—		
Charles Dalrymple of Hailes	33	130
Ayrshire—		
Countess of Stair	19,266	12,763
Countess of Stair (Mines)	—	852
Earl of Stair	492	940
	121,284	£83,221

Eighty-three thousand pounds per annum is a satisfactory dot. Is it the result of thrift, industry, saving, total abstinence, or genius, or is it the fruit of sycophantic greed, robbery, and cunning?

Let us see.

Away back in the fourteenth century the Dalrymples were small "bonnet lairds" in Ayrshire. About the year 1450 a certain William de Dalrymple married a relation of his, Agnes Kennedy, who was heiress to the lands of Stair Montgomery on the water of Ayr. The family was as yet comparatively poor, and was among the first to suffer persecution for adherence to and sympathy with the new heretical Protestant Lollard ideas that were disturbing the Church.

The first person of note in the family was James Dalrymple, who after studying at Glasgow, went to Edinburgh to the practice of law. Although of decided Protestant opinions, he seems to have been an adept at running with the hare and hunting with the hounds—especially the latter; and he was by no means averse to the pocketing of his principles when such a proceeding offered him certainty of advancement.

By his cunning and by his ability in the matter of keeping a foot in all camps, he rose rapidly in the legal profession. He was a Lord of Session under Cromwell, and President of the Court after the Restoration of Royalty. In the shifting scenes of the time he skipped from position to position with a dexterity that his contemporaries, Lord Arniston and the others, could not equal, and so he gradually became the most powerful legal personage in Scotland. Bishop Burnet, in his "History of My Own Time," says of Dalrymple that he was:–

> "A man of very mild deportment, but a false and cunning man and a great perverter of justice, in which he had a very particular dexterity of giving some plausible colours to the greatest injustice."

This perverter of justice married a Wigtonshire lady who brought with her a small estate at Carscreugh, near Glen Luce; but a cunning rascal of his description was not likely to long remain comparatively landless; and the family historian—Mr. Murray Graham—is constrained to admit in his annals of the Stairs that:–

> "Lord Stair (Dalrymple was a Lord now) made various additions to his estates of Stair and Carscreugh by new acquisitions of land, several of these being effected by recourse to the usual (sic) process in Scottish law whereby a creditor appraised or adjudged the debtors' lands, or a portion of them, for his debt, the lands so appraised becoming the property of the creditor if the debt were not redeemed within a certain time."*

From this one sees that there are still delicate and politic methods of describing the process of eating up widows' houses and grinding the faces of the poor.

What precisely were the Dalrymple land acquisition methods in Wigtonshire I do not know, but the family appears to have been enriched by the King with lands stolen from the Church. Mr. Graham states that in July, 1688, a Dalrymple purchased the estate of Castle Kennedy from John Lord Bargany; but, unless the Castle Kennedy estate was in no way connected with the lands of Glenluce Abbey, this must be a mistake. The story of this Glenluce Abbey property is a very interesting one, and indicates

---

* P. 52, Vol. I., "Annals of the Viscount and First and Second Earls of Stair." — J. Murray Graham.

the methods by which some of our noble families became "land magnates."

The Glenluce lands belonged to the Church, but a robber baron in the neighbourhood, one Gilbert, Earl of Cassilis (who shall be dealt with in another paper), cast covetous eyes on the property, and being, according to the family historian,

> "Ane particular man and ane greedy man, and cared
> not how he gat land so that he could come by the same,"†

he set upon the robbing of the Church. It seems that he had private negotiations set on foot with the Abbot, and had all but induced the Abbot to sign the necessary writs when the latter died. One might imagine that this would somewhat discomfit our Earl Gilbert; but not so. Remember that he was "ane particular and ane greedy man," and now let us turn to the family historian again.

> "And then he dealt with ane monk of the same Ab-
> bacy wha could counterfeit the Abbott's hand writ and
> all the haill convent, and gat him to counterfeit their
> subscriptions. When this was done, fearing that the
> monk might make unpleasant revelations, he gat a
> certain carl to 'stick' (stab) him, and then he got ane
> to accuse the carl of theft and hung him in Cronsgate,
> and so the lands of Glenluce were conquest."

Conquest!

Possibly he is right. It may be that the word conquest always carries in its bosom treachery, trickery, and theft.

Glenluce did not, however, long remain in Gilbert's hands, and after several "owners" had plundered it, it was again annexed to the Church in the See of Galloway. "Towards the end of the seventeenth century it was erected into a barony, and became the property of the noble family of Stair,"§ or to use less polite but

---

† "Histories of the Kennedies," p. 9.
§ Statistical Account of Scotland.

more truthful language, King Charles the Second robbed the Church and enriched the Dalrymples with his plunder. The Midlothian property of the Stair family, the Oxenford Castle property, and the Manor of Cousland, also belonged at one time to the Church. Who originally stole them from their owners, the monks of Kelso, I do not know, but it seems that a Dalrymple married them when he married an heiress of the Macgill family.

Some of the religious tests of his day offending Sir James Dalrymple, and his enemies getting the upper hand, he was obliged to fly to Holland. But if Sir James was gone, his son whom he left behind, appears judiciously to have become a leader of his fathers opponents, and the family of Dalrymple stood to gain no matter which side, Protestant or Catholic, Whig or Jacobite, was uppermost. Sir John became Lord Advocate, and persecuted the "hill-men" and crushed the "field conventicles" with the best. The family had a leader on both sides, and stood to win at all hazards. Says Lord Macaulay:–

> "During some months, Sir John at Edinburgh affected to condemn the disloyalty of his unhappy parent, Sir James; and Sir James at Leyden told his Puritan friends how deeply he lamented the wicked compliance of his unhappy child, Sir John."

The Revolution came, bringing with it as Macaulay says—"A large increase of wealth and honour to the House of Stair." The son deserted the Stuarts and adhered to King William (who had been successful). He was appointed Lord Advocate. His father was raised to the peerage, and the Dalrymples still swam with the tide.

In the year 1676 Sir James managed to get the City of Edinburgh to pay his house rent and that of his successors in office. This "privilege," one is glad to note, was politely refused by a succeeding president of the Court of Session, Duncan Forbes.

After reading some of the more or less savoury details of Sir James' career, I do not wonder that he spent the later years of his life writing an elaborate treatise entitled "A Vindication of the Divine Perfections, illustrating the Glory of God in them, by reason and revelation, methodically digested into several Meditations."

Every schoolchild knows the story of the awful massacre of Glencoe. The King, or as I take it, Mr. Secretary for Scotland Dalrymple, second Earl of Stair, had given timely warning to all the Highland Clans that unless they took the Oath of fealty to the new Protestant succession, there would be instituted a vigorous Highland campaign and a terrible revenge taken on the clansmen.

This oath of fealty had to be sworn by not later than the 1st of January 1692. Some few days before the expiry of the time limit, MacIan Macdonald of Glencoe, "with the most considerable men of his clan," appeared at Fort William to take the oath. Although the officer in charge at Fort William accepted the oath, he informed Macdonald that he (Macdonald) had not gone to the proper quarter. The Chief, to make matters secure, hurried off to Inverary, where he arrived a day too late. Sheriff Campbell, of Ardkinglass, however, again administered the oaths, and Macdonald departed for Glencoe, thinking all was well.

Shortly thereafter appears a company of soldiers in Glencoe—sent thither, they said, to be properly quartered because "the garrison of Inverlochy was thronged." The officers gave "their parole of honour that they would do neither him (Macdonald) nor his concerns any harm." Macdonald answered with true Highland generosity; for fifteen days he fed and housed the soldiers; the officers were his guests; and then—and then one windy, boisterous night Glencoe was enclosed, the passes guarded, and punctually at five o'clock in the morning the guests, acting on instructions, drew their swords and murdered the hapless Macdonalds as they slept. The orders were that none be spared who were under 70 years of age; nor was the Government to be troubled with prisoners; the Macdonalds were to be cut off root and branch; the hospitable clan had to be extirpated by the guests they had welcomed, and this by the King's command, instigated thereto of course by Stair. The houses were burned to the ground, the cattle driven off to the garrison of Inverlochy, where, we are told, the sheep and goats were divided among the officers; women with babes turned out into a vehement snowstorm, and there left to die! Two of the officers who had given their parole of honour to MacIan, and who had refused to be concerned in the treacherous murder, were sent as prisoners to Glasgow. It is one of the blackest crimes in British history, and we are glad to learn that it not only aroused intense indignation among the common people, but that the Scots Parliament demanded a Commission of Enquiry. Sir John Lowther, who had been offered the position of Lord Advocate of Scotland, refused the office because he would not be allowed to prosecute the murderers.

There is abundant evidence that the massacre was contrived and planned by Sir John Stair, who was at that time one of the Secretaries of Scotland, and trusted adviser of King William; though what precisely was Stair's motive for this ferocious and insensate treachery, cruelty and murder, I am unable to suggest. At any rate, on the 9th of January, Stair knew that MacIan had taken the oath; for in a letter of that date to Sir Thomas Levingston, he admitted it; but on the 11th January, he (Stair) issued the instructions for the massacre. Let me give some selections from Stair's letters of this time; they will indicate the humanitarian strain that must run in the family blood!

> "It's a great work of charity to be exact in rooting out that damnable sect."

> "The winter is the only season in which we are sure the Highlanders cannot escape us, nor carry their wives, bairns, and cattle to the mountains."

> ". . . This is the proper season to maul them in the cold long nights."

> "I hope the soldiers will not trouble the Government with prisoners."

"Pray when anything concerning Glenco is resolved, let it be secret and sudden. . . I think to herry their cattle, or burn their houses is but to render them desperate, lawless men to rob their neighbours. . . Argyll's detachment lies in Keappoch Well to assist the garison to do all on a sudden." ¶

A sort of compound of Genseric, Nero, Pizarro, and Abdul the Damned, this early founder of the fortunes of the house of Stair!

Fancy that human tiger appointed Secretary for Scotland; vision him licking his lean lawyer's chops over the massacre of the babes in Glencoe (I imagine he must have been lean of jaw and puny of stature, for was not this the ruffian whom the good Fletcher of Saltoun, one morning at the door of the Scots Parliament House, shook as a terrier does a rat?)

And what poor man of the Southland who touches his cap as the Stair carriage rolls by, or votes submissively to send Viscount Dalrymple to Parliament that he may obstruct and oppose Old Age Pensions for the aged toiler, or what poor housewife who pays rent, rent, rent, year in and year out from her meagre income in order to fatten and surfeit the idle Stairs—what poor man or woman of the Southland I ask, can have any respect or honour for a leisured and luxurious race that rose to wealth as the Stairs have done? The landscape gardening at Castle Kennedy is beautiful! Yes, but who paid for it? And the title to that endless exaction of rent! Ah, my friends, when you look at "the long avenue, smooth with close-cropped turf as a bowling green," remember the murdered babes of Glencoe and the legal sycophants whose cunning and duplicity founded the "nobility" of the Stairs.

¶ All the statements of fact about the Glencoe Massacre are taken from the most interesting of all Scots Histories, "The Memoirs of Viscount Dundee."

THE DUNDASES.

"A more despicable set of wretches cannot be found than the nobles of England under the Georges. Licentious, mean, in every way thoroughly corrupt and cruel, it would be difficult to find their superiors in the world's history."   —*J. A. Roebuck.*

"Scourged as was Shetland, by Royal favourites and greedy adventurers taking advantage of the unsuspecting and defenceless Udallers."
    Statistical Account of Scotland, Vol. 15, p. 155.

THE DUNDASES have two earldoms in their possession, and in the year 1874 had accumulated land spoil in Scotland as follows:–

	Acres.	Gross Annual Rental.
Earl of Leven and Melville—		
Fifeshire	1,019	£1,761
Edinburgh	1,158	3,618
Earl of Zetland—		
Fifeshire	5,566	8,339
Fifeshire (Mines)	—	832
Orkney	29,846	5,617
Clackmannan	2,726	3,27
Clackmannan (Mines)	—	2,635
Dumbartonshire	162	12
Stirling	4,656	9,552
Stirling (Mines)	—	4,256
Shetland	13,600	858
Colonel Joseph Dundas—		
Stirling	1,989	2,704
Stirling (Mines)	—	500
Dundas of Beechwood and Dunira		
Perthshire	5,529	2,725
Edinburgh	81	355
Peebles	22	10

Dundas of Arniston—		
Fifeshire	195	248
Fifeshire (Mines)	—	525
Edinburgh	10,184	9,549
Edinburgh (Mines)	—	4,254
Linlithgow	12	60
	73,745	£62,222

In addition to the above there are other Dundas landowners in Scotland, but as I cannot trace their relationship to the main stock, I have omitted them from my table.

Among these are the Right Hon. Sir David Dundas of Ochtertyre, who owns 984 acres in Perthshire with a rent-roll of £1231; Edward Thomas Dundas, of Manor, Stirling, who has only a beggarly 198 acres with a rent-roll of £400; the Hon. John C. Dundas, who appears in Linlithgowshire with 274 acres and annual rents of £409; and George Dundas, who figures in the same county with 2082 acres and £4723 in his rent-book. But that is by no means all.

The Earl of Zetland has got his clutches on much land in England (9623 acres in Yorkshire alone) and at least one of this noble family figures as an extractor of rent from the people of Ireland. In this series of articles, however, I am dealing only with our "noble" families in as far as they are a curse to Scotland, the histories of the English nobility having been adequately dealt with elsewhere.*

The earliest Dundas we have any accurate knowledge of was one John Dundas of Dundas, "who was in high favour" at the Court of King James the Third. He was, indeed, so far in "high favour" that he extracted a promise from the King that he, Dundas, would be created Earl of Forth. The King, however, was killed before he could implement his promise, and so poor John Dundas got no handle to his name.

---

* See "Our Old Nobility,"—Howard Evans.

It was from this Court *mouchard* that the Dundases were descended. The only other reliable piece of information we have about him is that one of his sons was knighted in order to properly celebrate the baptism of Prince Henry, and that it is this knighted individual whom the Irish landlord Dundases worship as their progenitor.

Let us glance quickly at the Arniston branch. The first outstanding gentleman of this section was a governor of the town of Berwick. This Governor's eldest son was knighted by the dissolute and debauched King, Charles II. He contrived to be elected as M.P. for the County of Edinburgh, and after the due and proper period had elapsed, was "raised" to the peerage as Lord Arniston. It is strange—passing strange—how even in these corrupt days of the Merry Monarch, the legal spoils of Scotland ran steadily to the Dundases of Arniston. Lord Arniston's son (how strange!) also became M.P. for the County of Edinburgh; he was a lawyer and became a judge. But we are not at the strange part yet. This judge's son *also* became M.P. for the County of Edinburgh; he *also* became a judge; incidentally he became also Lord Advocate and President of the Court of Session. Still is the story incomplete, for did not this Court of Session President, have a son and did not *he also* become M.P. for Edinburgh and Lord President and Solicitor-General and Lord Advocate! This brings us up to the year 1754. Now this last Lord Advocate, M.P., etc., had *four* sons and it was impossible that they could all be appointed to the lucrative positions aforementioned. Of course the jobs might have been divided among the cubs, but that would have destroyed the Dundas tradition for keeping all the legal plums in the chief branch of the family, and so *for the fifth time in succession* all these offices fell to the eldest Dundas. But did the aged parent calmly allow his other three sons to starve? Not he! One was appointed Lieutenant General and Governor of the Cape of Good Hope; another was appointed Lord Clerk Registrar of Scotland; and the remaining son had to be content with the Governorship of the Prince of Wales Island. The tender Burke, in his "Peerage," naively declares that this continual family inheritance of important State offices "seems to be without a parallel," and leaves the matter at that; but a generation is arising which is not impressed with the device of condoning jobberies by merely covering them up with innocuous and pleasant sounding phrases.

Let us, however, return to the history of the fifth of the generation of legal Brahmins; for in him was the outrageous corruption of his family so exemplified that at last an enraged (and even in itself anything but honest) House of Commons demanded his impeachment. Had he been content with the usual family spoil, his descendants might still have been Lord High Everything except Honest at Edinburgh; but he aspired to greater things; his fingers yearned for bigger pilferings, and being a confidant of Pitt (who was often exceeding careless in the choice of his political bedfellows), he was raised to the peerage in 1802 as Baron Dunira and Viscount Melville. He was received into the Cabinet, and when already holding high office there, he secured appointment as Privy Seal of Scotland; he wheedled himself into a grant of the Stewardship of Fife, and after receiving this appointment, his voracity was so great that he exacted "arrears of salary" amounting to £3000, arrears which the very people who signed the warrants, declared they knew nothing of. For his wife he managed to grab a pension of £1500 per annum; and indeed he showed himself such a beast of prey on the public purse that Fox did not at all exaggerate matters when he described him as a man who

> "ever showed an eagerness to heap up emoluments,
> and systematise corruption."

It is almost impossible in cold print to portray the feeling of disgust and aversion that surges through the investigator as he follows the money maniac Melville through the histories of the period. As despot and enemy of public freedom, he shows himself at almost every turn; but it is as thief at the national money bags that we must deal with him here. He had managed to capture the three offices of

Minister of War, President of the Board of Control, and Treasurer of the Navy. It was well known that previous "Lords" had reaped glorious harvests in the last-named office by the simple expedient of keeping large sums of the public funds lying at some of the banks, and, with these sums, doing a huge private business in the discounting of bills, and occasionally dipping into stock speculations.

When Melville was appointed to the office of Treasurer of the Navy, he was so anxious to disarm his enemies that he made this lucrative swindling illegal. Such a proposal coming from a man with Dundas's record should have rendered the House of Commons suspicious; but it appears to have been so gratified at the possibility of his possessing some regard for the public purse, that it raised his salary from £2000 to £4000. Still, ugly rumours soon got abroad, and in the year 1803 Parliament appointed a Commission of Inquiry to probe into the "alleged malversation" of the public funds by Melville and his satellite and accomplice, Alexander Trotter. This Trotter appears to have been a clerk in the Navy Office at a salary of £50 a year, with a "slowly rising increment" when Melville came across him. Melville got him appointed as his deputy at an annual salary of £500, which was afterwards raised to £800; and thereafter the worthy pair commenced a systematic public plundering. In the year 1802 Trotter's "profits" from stock he had "acquired" were £11,308, and he had invested largely in land. Before the Commission of Inquiry he admitted he was now "worth" £65,000. Actually how far Lord Melville had profited by these nefarious transactions, it is impossible to say, *as immediately before the trial Melville and Trotter burned documents and accounts for* £134,000,000 *of public money which had passed through their hands*. Melville naturally protested his innocence, but it was proved up to the hilt that some of the money given by Trotter to Melville had been invested in stock in Melville's name, and after Melville had been heard in his own defence at the bar of the House of Commons, William Wilberforce was so disgusted that he declared the defence "was but an aggravation of his guilt." Melville, of course, was forced to resign all his offices, and his name was deleted from the Privy Council list. He was ultimately tried by the House of Lords on ten different counts, but was acquitted by majorities ranging from 27 to 137. Dr. Morrison Davidson, in referring to these decisions, quotes the old Scots proverb, that "one corbie does not pick out another corbie's een," and Miss Martineau in her history declares it "impossible that many, if any, should believe him actually innocent of the charges brought against him."

These events happened in the palmy days of aristocratic rascality, when the common lands of the people were being stolen and enclosure acts were being passed not in units but in battalions. It is not, therefore, surprising to find that on Melville's death, his widow was given a pension of £1000 per annum, and that his family with an effrontery almost unsurpassed, had got themselves quartered on the public purse. One son was First Lord of the Admiralty. The second Earl was Lord Privy Seal of Scotland with an annual salary of £2675. His sister, Lady Elizabeth, held a pension of £300 for fifty-one years; his eldest son was at once a general, a colonel, and a governor of Edinburgh Castle; his second son became Lord of the Admiralty with a wage for doing nothing of £10,000 a year; his third son, says Burke's "Peerage," was Storekeeper General of the Navy (salary not stated); his fourth son went in for Divinity, and collared a "living" of £988 and a free manse. It is not, therefore, altogether inappropriate that the present holder of the title should have represented the King at the opening of the Church of Scotland's annual assembly.

Generations of Melvilles nowadays seem to have fallen on (comparatively) evil times; and the Consular Service, it appears, is all that is left to them. The present Earl has served in some diplomatic capacity or other at Hamburg and Christiana, and his son has been Vice-Consul at Algiers, Assistant District Officer in British East Africa, etc.

Now we go on to another branch of the family, the Earl of Zetland. He is descended from one Thomas Dundas of Fingask, who appears about the year 1740 to have been M.P. for Orkney and Shetland.

This Thomas Dundas had a descendant, Sir Lawrence Dundas, who was "Commissary General and Contractor to the Army" from 1748-1759. Army contractors in these days were frequently tarry-fingered gentry; indeed, Dr. Morrison Davidson in his picturesque way describes them as "great public robbers"; but whether or not Sir Lawrence emulated his relative, the Treasurer of the Navy, I am unable to say. At any rate he appears to have "succeeded" in life, for we find him in the year 1776 paying no less a sum that £66,000 for lands in Orkney and Shetland—buying thereby stolen property, as we shall immediately see. Sir Lawrence's son was created Baron Dundas of Aske, and this Baron's son, who performed some possibly imaginary services as "Vice Admiral of Orkney and Shetland," was created first Earl of Zetland. The present Earl is the happy possessor of three titles, Earl of Zetland, Earl of Ronaldshay, and Baron Dundas, and takes his seat occasionally in the House of Lords—usually on such occasions as on the Licensing Bill debate, when of course he voted to give the Commons' measure no consideration whatsoever.

Let us look at the history of the lands this family holds in Orkney and Shetland. Even *in cameo* as I give it, it throws a lurid light on the methods by which our large landowning families acquired their territory. The following quotation is from the "New Statistical Account of Scotland," Vol. 15, pages 61-62 (portion devoted to the parishes of Tingwall, Whiteness, and Weesdale); and is written by the Rev. John Turnbull, Parish Minister. I have taken the liberty of italicising some words and phrases.

> "By a treaty of 1470 Shetland was pledged to the Crown of Scotland *; and from that period, the original inhabitants were most grievously oppressed by tyrants from time to time sent over by the Scottish Crown. At the time of the transfer, all the property in Shetland was held by Udal tenure (descending from father to son without any written documents), *paid no fees, and owned no superior.*

---

* From Norway

"About 1664 Douglas of Spynie, factor for Lord Grandison, compelled many of the simple Udallers to take out feu-charters for their lands. Very few of the Norwegians now possess lands in Shetland. There are still a few in Dunrossness and Cunningsburgh. For a century before the Islands were transferred to the Scottish Crown, the St Clairs of Caithness possessed a very large share of the Shetland property, which their descendants enjoyed until a late period.

"In 1530 the Islanders were so oppressed by James, Earl of Moray, that simple and yielding as they were, *they rose in arms against his factor, and the Crown was compelled to revoke the charter granted to him of the lands belonging to it in Shetland.*

"In 1561 Queen Mary, importuned by Lord Robert Stewart, her natural brother, made a grant to him of all the Crown lands in Orkney and Shetland. After her unfortunate connection with Bothwell, she revoked the grant given to Lord Robert Stewart and conferred it on her husband. On Bothwell's forfeiture, the lands again reverted to the Crown, and Lord Robert Stewart gained possession of them, but *owing to his cruelty to the inhabitants, he was deprived of them, and confined for six months in the Palace of Linlithgow.* But in 1581 his interest at Court procured for him a new grant of the Earldom; he was also appointed Justiciar with power to convoke and dissolve Lawtainings. *He forfeited the grant in 1585.* In 1587 Sir John Maitland obtained a grant of the islands, revenues, etc.; but having resigned, Lord Robert Stewart prevailed on King James to confer them on him; and in 1600 Earl Patrick† obtained a new grant of them, lived at Scalloway, built the castle, and *grievously* oppressed the inhabitants, doing all in his power to prevent their complaints reaching the ears of the Government. In 1608, however, they made known their grievances to Parliament, which in 1612, revoked the charter and annexed the lordship to the

---

† Patrick Stewart, son of Lord Robert.

Crown. Two years afterwards Earl Patrick, who *justly merited punishment for his cruelty to the Shetlanders*, was put to death for high treason. He had the power of life and death over the inhabitants of these islands, fined them, *and confiscated their property at his pleasure*. He assessed the country in money, provisions, and personal labour. He also feued lands *he had seized from the poor Udallers;* and these with scatt and other burdens imposed, together with the Crown lands, form the revenue of the Earldom of Shetland.

"In 1614 Sir James Stewart of Ochiltree farmed the Crown property, but he being also *guilty of the greatest oppression*, was deprived of it.

"In 1624 Sir George Hay was appointed Farmer General and Steward of the Islands. He, too, *oppressed the poor Shetlanders*; and the Lordship was again annexed to the Crown by Act of Parliament.

"In the reign of Charles I, the Earl of Morton obtained a wadset of the Lordship of Shetland and Earldom of Orkney for the sum of £30,000, said to have been advanced His Majesty by him. This deed was ratified by Act of Parliament. No attention was paid to it during the Commonwealth; but at the Restoration, Viscount Grandison, as trustee for the Morton Family, obtained a grant of the property and revenues belonging to the Crown in Shetland and Orkney.

"In 1641 *the alleged debt* due the Earl of Morton was discharged, and the Lordship of Shetland and the Earldom of Orkney were to remain inseparably annexed to the Crown. During the reign of Queen Anne, however, on account of the active part taken by James, Earl of Morton, in bringing about the Union between England and Scotland, he obtained a new grant in the form of a wadset, redeemable for the old sum of £30,000.

"In 1742 the Earl of Morton obtained an irredeemable right to the lands, on condition of improving the Islands. He was to drain marshes, build harbours, promote the fisheries, and improve the agriculture. *These conditions, however, have never been fulfilled.*

"In 1776 Lord Morton sold his lands and casualties in Shetland to Sir Lawrence Dundas, the ancestor of the present Earl of Zetland, for the sum of £66,000."

So that since the conditions under which Morton got the land were never fulfilled, the lands of the Zetland family in the Islands do not legally belong to them but belong to the Crown. Perhaps some day when we have a democratic Government, there will be such an examination of title deeds that land nationalisation may arrive in places without much talk of compensation.

After the Dundases had bought the stolen property from the Mortons, matters did not improve much, so far as the peasantry were concerned. The Rev. John Bryden, minister of Standsting and Aithsting, tells us that:–

"Even when subject to a milder sway, the acts of former oppressors continued to be felt; and many exactions, equally unjust in themselves, and contrary to express stipulations, were made and continued to be made; these, by prescription, having become legal demands."

It was only in the year 1829, that Scatt, an iniquitous form of Danish land tax, was added to the people's burden; and it is only in comparatively recent times that the infamous "Jus Primæ Noctis," by which the landlord took or could take legal priority with young married women, was swept away from Orkney. The Rev. Mr. Turnbull mentions another custom only lately deceased, that of taking "some young boys" at appointed times to the marches and bestowing on them "a good flogging at particular places, in order that they might remember the marches; after which they received some little reward"!

Landlordism appears to have been a positive boon to the islanders, doesn't it?

THE ATHOLLS

AND THE TREASURY.

"A robber band has seized the land,
And we are exiles here."   —*Edward Carpenter.*

AT THE TIME of the last Landowners' Return (1874) the Duke of Atholl was given as the "owner" of 194,640 acres in Perthshire, rental £40,758; and in the year 1908 a Parliamentary Return was issued showing that the Duke of Atholl was the largest "owner" of deer forests in the non-crofting Counties of Scotland. The following official figures should arouse us to the enormous extent to which the deer forest has banished the agriculturist in the non-crofting Counties:–

Scots Deer Forests not in the Crofting Counties.

	Area.	Rental.
Duke of Fife	87,000	£4000
Duke of Richmond	72,000	3410
Lord Dalhousie	26,600	1600
Duke of Atholl	91,700	6955
Lord Tullibardine	14,500	1010
Sir Neil Menzies, Bart.	52,000	3805
King Edward	16,000	1000

Father Atholl and son Tullibardine, it will be seen, have secured over 106,000 acres for their "sport," and they have, it will be observed, managed to screw down the rental thereon to a matter of £7965, or about 1/6 per acre per annum. But one can be assured that although these worthies assess the ground they "use"

41

themselves at a paltry 1/6 per acre, they will not be so lenient to feuars.

The history of the Stewart-Murrays reads like an Arabian romance of successful crime. The first of the race, one Freskin, a Fleming, appears to have been a prosperous pirate, doing business on a large scale. Burke's "Peerage" declares that this Freskin, in the 12th century, "owned extensive lands in Moray and Strathbrock in Linlithgow." Freskin appears to have been deputed to "subdue" the men of Moray, and he appears to have stuck closely to the lands of the subdued people. The family fortunes were frequently enriched by successful marriages—the lands of Gask and Tullibairn (or Tullibardine) being thus acquired. One of the Tullibardines obtained the office of Hereditary Sheriff of Perthshire, and when this office was abolished it is highly probable that heavy compensation was demanded and secured. They appear to have been, indeed, a "noble" family. One, at least, was hung as a traitor; one attempted to emulate King Charles II and leave a dozen illegitimate children to be supported by the nation, but he had only managed eight at the time of his death; another Stewart-Murray "obtained the lands of Lethendy and Cultran-ioch" ("obtained" is the official word); and the family became notorious for its genius in the art of jumping down on the right side of the fence in the various treasons and plots of the Stuart period.

The Atholl crest is "a demi-savage proper holding in his right hand a dagger." The original designer of that crest was seemingly a man who believed in literal accuracy. And the most virulent critic of our hereditary rent-drawers and land-grabbers could never honestly deny that the Atholl family motto of "Furth Fortune and fill the fetters" had been scrupulously acted up to; the only unfortunate thing being that it was always other people who filled the fettters. Let us lift merely one curtain in the history of the "Noble" Atholls; let us see the noble family at work at the "furth fortune business," filling their pockets from the public treasury.

In the year 1406, in the reign of Henry IV, one John de Stanley, ancestor of the house of Derby, obtained a grant of the Lordship of the Isle of Man, on condition that he paid a fixed rent of £101 15/11 to the Crown. The revenues were worth at that time £400 a year, so that John de Stanley had landed into a nice little sinecure of £300 a year. After this plunder had gone on for some 350 years, the Crown desired to purchase the "office" back again; and it was then discovered that it had been long acquired (through marriage) by the Duke of Atholl. Already for 359 years a minimum of £300 a year, equal to £107,700 had been paid; but the Duke would not let his "rights" go for less than £70,000 cash down, a sum ultimately if reluctantly agreed to. At the time of purchase, revenues from the Isle of Man were certainly not, according to Lord Ellenborough, more than £800 a year. It will be seen that fortune had gone furth, and the Duke and Duchess wrote expressing undoubted "satisfaction" with the bargain made, as indeed well they might. But soon after this Ducal Cormorant wrote asking *for a further pension of* £2,000 *on the lives of himself and his Duchess,* and this was granted, and by the year 1805 another £100,000 had been paid on this Isle of Man "job," thus making the total up to £277,700.

The worst is yet to come. Seven years after the Duke was dead, his son had the impertinence to apply for further compensation; but even a house of landlords, engaged themselves in little "Jobs," could not for very shame's sake but refuse. Seven years later he tried the same dodge, but William Pitt would have none of it. Fourteen years later, his Parliamentary support being required by the Government of the day, and he himself seeing that the lobbies were well canvassed, he made a third attempt, and this time succeeded in getting for the Atholl Family *one-fourth of the revenues of the Isle of Man for all time to come.*

This was in 1804. His share of the Isle of Man spoil at that time amounted to £3000 per annum, with every prospect of increase as trade and industry developed; and he continued drawing his fourth share till 1825. That is to say, he collared for 21 years a minimum sum of £3000, or £63,000; *thus raising the total plunder to* £340,700. This scandalous fraud did not, however, pass without severe opposition. Earl Temple and Mr. Windham denounced the thing as a "scandalous" job; Lord Eldon (then Lord Chancellor) declared it was a "dangerous precedent" and the Duke of Clarence (afterwards King William IV) and the Duke of Norfolk went boldly into the voting lobbies against it.

Then in 1825, when the Reform Bill was on the horizon, Parliament decided that this shameful robbery must be stopped, and we find in Burke's "Peerage" that the then Duke "disposed" of his property and privileges in the isle of Man to the Crown for the sum of £400,000. Add the £340,700 already paid, and you have thus the magnificent total on this single job of £740,000. Three-quarters of a million pounds! And meantime no talk of the Atholl family being publicly ostracised till they make restitution!

The Earl of Mansfield is also a Murray, being descended from the Sir William Murray of Tullibardine, who flourished about 1507. The Mansfield branch holds lands as follows:–

	Area.	Rental.
Dumfries-shire: Lord Mansfield	14,342	£13,389
Perthshire	31,197	23,052
Clackmannanshire	1,705	3,617
	472,244	£40,058

These estates are the fruit of successful alliances with heiresses, and a steady begging at Court. Sir David Murray of Gospertie, for example, managed to secure in royal grants the barony of Segy (1601); Falkland, with the office of Ranger of the Lowmonds and forester of the woods (1601); Glendovick (1602); Balinblae and Muthill (1602); Ruthven (1602)—and he also added to his possessions the lands belonging to the Abbacy of Scone, which were evidently dismembered by the King for the benefit of his favourite.

The only Murray of this branch who rose to any eminence

was the lawyer who became first Lord Mansfield. He was one of the genuine reactionaries of his time; was a powerful advocate of the policy that lost us the American Colonies; did his best to get Wilkes outlawed; and, finally, he so outraged public opinion that in 1780 a mob burned his house in London, Mansfield only escaping with his life.*

The Earl of Dunmore is also a Murray, being descended from the second son of the first Marquis of Atholl. He owns:

	Area.	*Rental.*
Inverness-shire	60,000	£2,339
Stirlingshire	4,620	8,922

The Dunmore branch have simply been undistinguished rent collectors.

---

* The Nova Scotia Baronetcy hoax is explained in the paper on the Erskine Family.

THE DUFFS

SUCCESSFUL PETTY KNAVERY.

"On the one hand Lord Fife is pushing us into the sea, and on the other, Lord Seafield jams us close to the river."
—*Rev. Wm. Grant, p. 48, Vol. 13, Stat. Ac. of Scotland.*

"The interest of the landlord is always opposed to the interest of every other class in the community."
—*Ricardo.*

"Plinius found in large landed properties the cause of Italy's ruin."
—*Flurscheim "Clue to the Economic Labyrinth," p. 28.*

The Scotsman objected to the American that America was not much of a country because it had no nobility.
"And what be 'nobility' ?" asked the Yank.
"Oh—er—gentlemen who don't work," replied the Scot.
"Ow," said the Yank, cheerfully, "we have 'em; only we call 'em tramps."

THE DUKE of Fife, who, by the way, owns no land in Fife, does not come of a race of filibustering and murderous pirates, like some of the blue-blooded gentry whose histories we have been dealing with. Wild Mahratta-like rapine and blood-shed are not characteristics of the Duffs; they have specialised in cunning, in legal trickery, in underhand dodgery, in the calm and determined appropriation of common lands and church lands. Successful marriages have been a decided feature of the family history, and the present Duke of Fife has only gone one better than his ancestors, when he married into the Royal Family. The Duffs were originally petty lairds on the Aberdeenshire and Banffshire borders, and the founders of the house are declared in Burke's "Peerage" to have been wonderfully diligent in the adding of field to field.

In due course, and by methods which I shall detail later on, the Duffs amassed great wealth; they bought up many lands (they also got lands without undue emphasis being laid on the buying up); they raised themselves to the peerage with the title of Lord Braco; they were never attainted for rebellion—they were too cunning for that; when estates were forfeited, the Duff lands were never among them; when "Bloody Cumberland" went North after the Rebellion, a Duff was ready to do "anything" he was desired, possibly with a keen eye on the forfeited estates of the Jacobite nobles; and so when the last Landowners' Return was prepared, the Duffs appear smiling with the following accumulation of acres to their credit:–

Aberdeenshire—	*Acres.*	*Gross Annual Rental.*
Garden A. Duff	11,576	£9,661
Major Duff	4,328	2,356
W. E. Grant Duff	1,013	1,294
R. W. Duff	1,588	1,747
Grant Duff of Greenness	913	302
Duff of Corsindae	4,481	2,171
Earl of Fife	139,829	17,740
Banffshire—		
Duff of Drummuir	13,053	7,418
W. E. Grant Duff	7	20
R. W. Duff	2,671	2,346
Earl of Fife (Harbour)	5	500
Earl of Fife (Harbour)	5	500
Elginshire—		
Duff of Fochabers	3,019	1,793
Major Duff	5	86
Duff of Hopeman	552	587

Duff of Hopeman (Harbour)	2	72
Earl of Fife	40,959	18,693
	296,028	£102,665

Precisely how these lands were come by, we can only guess, but a few stray indications in the "Statistical Account of Scotland" may assist us in arriving at an approximately correct estimate of the Duff methods.

Prior to the year 1470 the lands and fishings belonging to the town of Banff were communally owned. Even in that year when "for the theicking of the kirk with slate," and other purposes, it was decided to let out the fishings to individual burgesses, great care was taken to see that the leases were only given for 19 years. Nowadays everything is gone. At the time of the Reformation, when hungry barons eyed the lands of the church, the Carmelite Brethren in Banff feued out part of their lands at a small duty. To-day not only part, but all the lands then feued south of the town are, somehow or other, in the possession of the Earl of Fife. The superiority and feu-duties which in the year 1617, had been gifted by James VI to King's College, Aberdeen, have also, it appears, been secured by the Duff Family. The fishings in the river, hitherto owned by *all* the people, now yield Lord Fife over £1600 per annum.

At the time the Statistical Account was written, the town of Banff had a small fishing on the west side of the town from which it drew an annual rent of £191. But the Earl of Fife was even then entering upon some legal devilment or other by which he hoped to grab even this annual rent. I cannot come across any account showing whether he was successful or not.

In the Statistical Account the Rev. Wm. Todd, minister of Alvah, complains that the lands of Kirktown were donated in 1375 to the church for all time coming, by an ancestor of the present Duke of Fife, and that:–

> "*it is a very curious fact* that he should be in possession

at the present day of the lands which were given away
by his ancestor."

A very curious fact, says our simple minister. Alas! I fear he can be
but ill-acquainted with the thieving propensities of the noble Duffs.

The following quotation from the late parish minister of
Grange should throw some light on the subject:–

> "Grange was feued out into small lairdships, upon
> the appearance of the Reformation, by the then Ab-
> bot of Kinloss, and was thus put into the hands of a
> great number of small proprietors. In the course of
> years, the number diminished, as the wealth of some
> and the wants of others increased. It is said of Alex-
> ander Duff of Braco, Lord Fife's ancestor, one of the
> more cautious and economical of the feuars, that as
> he was standing on the hillside at his residence of
> Braco, and seeing many of the laird's chimneys smok-
> ing around him, he remarked to a bystander, that he
> would make the smoke of these houses all go through
> one vent by and bye; and he nearly accomplished his
> purpose, as four-fifths of the whole are now in the
> hands of his descendants."

Imlach, in his "History of Banff" (p.10), tells us how the
town of Banff, which had much common land out on feu among
the burgesses, at "short lets" of 19 years, was forced to sell out
such lands or feu them out perpetually or hand them over peacably
to private persons. The town applied for a charter giving permission
to sell its common lands on 9th May 1581, and in the preamble it is
declared that when the 19 years' leases run out "*the nobility in the
neighbourhood, seeing the same and hoping to acquire the profits, did trouble
and molest the peace of the town and give no rest to the people.*" In this
Charter the king, "in order," as we are told, "to preserve the
Government of the town pure from any mixture of the aristocracy,
gives power to the Council to dispose of their property to residing
burgesses and their heirs male only." From which it will be seen
that the king evidently knew the gentry the people of Banff were

likely to be troubled with. But Charter or none, the Duffs have acquired some three-fourths of this land, and at least two of the methods of acquisition will hardly bear scrutiny. The first method, mentioned by Imlach, was the old dodge of shifting forward a boundary wall and sneaking all the new land thus enclosed. The other method was the acquisition of lands by the noble Duff through the medium of his factor and relative, one Archibald Duff, who had managed to get himself elected a Provost. This worthy induced the needy burgesses to sell out, and of course the "Noble" Duff was always behind his kinsman.

The story of how the Duffs stole the lands of Edinaich has been told in detail in a little booklet issued by the Henderson and Ogilvie Memorial Committee, which I may briefly summarise.

Away back in the reign of King Edward I there were schools in the larger towns in Scotland. A compulsory Education Act was passed in 1496, and about the beginning of the 17th century the Privy Council of Scotland interested itself greatly in the promotion of education facilities.

In the year 1647, a writer in Edinburgh – one Alexander Ogilvie – for, as he said:–

> "the love and affection which I have to learning and virtuous education of children within the parochin of Keith where I was born and bred"

left his estate of Edinaich near Keith, Banffshire, as a perpetual source of revenue, for all time coming, to the education authorities of Keith.

The estate was about 200 acres in extent. "From 1648 to 1687," says the "Prospectus of the Keith Grammar School," issued by the Keith School Board for the year 1908-1909, "the successive schoolmasters were in unquestioned enjoyment of the lands." But in the year 1687, Lord Braco, a progenitor of the present Duke of Fife, managed to get the schoolmaster (who had no legal power to sign away the land) to hand it over to him in return for a "consideration," which consideration Braco, of course, chose to forget. Year after year, generation after generation, the local Kirk Session pled with Braco for return of the lands, but to no effect. Latterly in 1827 a local schoolmaster, James Smith, managed to stir up public feeling, and £340 was locally subscribed to take the matter to the Court of Session, whereupon it was seen that the Duke of Fife had (nominally, at least), handed the estate over to the Earl of Seafield. But the case went on, and parties were heard before Lord Moncrieff in the year 1830, who made avizandum. *It was three years afterwards before Lord Moncrieff gave his decision, and during the time of the action the Duke of Fife was busy mortgaging the estate.* Moncrieff's decision ought to have been immediately appealed against, for he upheld the Duke of Fife's claim on the ground of prescription, *i.e.*, that the estate had been held by his family for a sufficient number of years.

THE SCOTTS OF BUCCLEUGH

BANDIT CHIEF TO DUKEDOM.

"Those transparent swindles—transmissible nobility
and kingship." —*Mark Twain.*

"Nature had appointed neither him, nor me, nor anyone else as lord of this particular land."
—*Horace "Satires"Book 2, p.* 129.

"Idlers, game-preservers, and mere human clothes-
horses." —*Carlyle.*

I DO not know if the late Charles Peace, Esq., Jack the Ripper, or
Pritchard the Poisoner, left issue behind them to perpetuate the
glory of their name and works; but if they did, I am certain that the
said issue feel profoundly ashamed of the stock from which they
sprung, and have sought diligently to efface the memory of their
ancestors.

Not so the Scotts of Buccleugh. Descended from Border
thieves, land pirates and freebooters, they still boast their pedigree.
The blood of knaves and moonlighters has by process of snobbery
become blue blood; lands raped from the weak and the unfortunate
now support arrogance in luxury; a position attained by the pikes
of the peasantry is used to oppress the poor.

The following is, so far as I can trace it, the land held by the
Buccleugh family in Scotland in the year 1874. There are other
Scotts perhaps who ought to be included, Scott of Ardvourlie in
Inverness-shire, for example, who has bagged almost 60,000 acres;

but I cannot connect him with the main stock. Indeed, these Buccleugh Scotts have so scattered their fledglings, have so intermarried them, and generally mixed them up, that I am in doubt if one or two of the smaller landowners I give in my table ought not to be included in some other noble nest:–

	Acres.	Gross Annual Rental.
Berwickshire—		
Lord Polwarth	4,714	6,843
Lady Alicia Scott	11,412	5,425
Dumfriesshire—		
Duke of Buccleugh and Queensbury	253,514	94,518
Duke of Buccleugh and Queensbury (Mines)	–	3,012
Earl of Dalkeith	25	35
Scott of Raeburn	4,500	1,300
Lord Walter Scott	32	55
Scott of Watcarrick	1,054	300
Edinburgh County—		
Duke of Buccleugh	3,532	16,216
Duke of Buccleugh (Mines)	–	1,479
Duke of Buccleugh (Granton Harbour)	9	10,601
Duke of Buccleugh (Edinburgh Town)	4	112
Scott of Malleny	3,250	3,964
Fifeshire—		
Duke of Buccleugh and Queensberry	60	15
Forfarshire—		
Lady Scott of Balgay	300	1,328
Haddingtonshire—		
Lord Polwarth	1,848	2,361
Kirkcudbrightshire—		
Duke of Buccleugh	1,000	100
Lanarkshire—		
Duke of Buccleugh	9,091	1,544
Peebleshire—		
Duke of Buccleugh	248	272
Earl of Dalkeith	24	46
Lord H. Scott	24	45

Roxburghshire—		
Duke of Buccleugh	104,487	39,457
Lord Polwarth	4,102	5,280
Scotts of Howcleugh, Langlee,		
Overwells, Abbotsford,		
Ricalton, Wauchope, Ancrum,		
Hopetoun, etc.	15,000	13,500
Selkirkshire—		
Duke of Buccleugh	60,428	19,828
Lord Polwarth	3,595	1,760
Scotts of Howcleuch, Gala,		
Wauchope, and Sinton	9,378	6,440
	492,131	£235,836

The total comprises an area as large as Lanarkshire.

The earliest Scott we have any accurate knowledge of was one Richard le Scott, evidently, if we may judge by his name, of Norman extraction. This Richard married the heiress of Murthockston and Rankilburn, and either he or his brother appears on the infamous "Ragman Rolls" as having sworn to betray Scotland to Edward I of England.

The estates were slowly added to. The expulsion of the Maxwells from Eskdale, the Beatties from Ewsdale, and the downfall of the Earl of Bothwell added largely to the Scott lands.

Sir Walter Scott tells us in verse* of the shameful methods by which the Beatties (or Beattisons) were rooted out. Lord Morton, the feudal Superior, one day impudently demanded of a Beattison that he should give him his

". . . Best steed as a vassal ought."

But the Beattison, instead of meekly complying, threatened to crack his Lordship's pate; and that gentleman, with fierce desire for revenge in his heart, set off for the robber castle of Buccleugh. On arrival there, he spluttered out:–

---

* "Lay of the Last Minstrel," Canto IV. Stanzes 10-12

". . . Take these traitors to thy yoke;
For a cast of hawks and a purse of gold,
All Eskdale I'll sell thee to have and hold."

Scott, we are told, was "a glad man," and set off with his followers to subdue the Beattisons. His idea of subjection was expressed in his slaying every Beattison with one exception.

"The Scotts have scattered the Beattison clan,
In Eskdale they left but one landed man."

About the years 1420-1446, the Inglis who held Branxholm exchanged it for the lands of Murthockston which lay somewhat outside the regular routes of bloody murder and cattle stealing; but the Scott of the period declared that the "cattle in Cumberland were as good as those in Teviotdale." It was an easy bargain for the Scotts, as was also the one driven with the Monks of Kelso, whereby the Abbey parted with the lands of Bellendean for those of Glenkerry. After the Battle of Arkinholm, when the revolt of the Douglases was crushed, the King rewarded the Scotts who had fought on his side with much Douglas land—Eckford, Quitchester, lands at Crawfordjohn, and lands in the forests of Ettrick and Selkirk are specially mentioned.† About 1469 David Scott was appointed Laird of Buccleugh as a henchman to the Earl of Angus, and was given bailieship and landwardenship over Liddesdale, Ewesdale, and Eskdale. Instead of being mere harriers of English cattle, land acquisitors, and freebooters, the Scotts now, with their newly-found powers, developed a great passion for law and order. The wild untameable clans who lived nomad fashion, "plundering fat purses that went by" in the debatable lands that separated Scotland from England, were hounded from pillar to post by the Scotts, who probably had keen eyes for increased tracts of land. It is no part of my business to whitewash the "reputit thieves and broken men" of the debatable lands, but there is this to be said for them, that they had a code of honour unknown to

---

† "Upper Teviotdale," J. R. Oliver, p. 70.

the respectable freebooter who now wielded King's authority. Says Bishop Lesley§:–

> "They have a persuasion that all property is common by the law of nature."

They only took what they considered necessary, and believed that in so doing they were acting in accordance with divine law.

> "They never said their prayers with more fervour of devotion than when bound on some plundering expedition."

They avoided the shedding of blood unless it was done to revenge some insult or injury.

> "Violated confidence or trust they regarded as the greatest crime a man could be guilty of; and a Borderer would rather have suffered death than incur the odium attaching to one who had broken faith."¶

For a time Buccleugh harried the "broken-men" with great severity, but having stolen certain of the Queen's Jointure lands in Ettrick Forest, he got into trouble himself, and was shortly afterwards publicly accused of being in alliance with all the freebooter and banditti chiefs.

The next Laird of Buccleugh appears to have been a King's man, for his name appears in the list of those who gathered spoil at the downfall of the Earl of Angus in 1528. About this time began that long family feud between the Kers and the Scotts, which resulted in perpetual Border warfare for many generations. Selkirk was burned by the Kers for no other reason than that their hated enemy, Buccleugh, was Provost, and the quarrel was carried even to the streets of Edinburgh, where Buccleugh was stabbed. For several generations more there is little to record of the Scotts beyond feud, raid, foray, broil, and cattle-lifting. Here they "received" some land from the

---

§ See "Border Antiquities," Vol. II., App. No. 6
¶ "Upper Teviotdale," p. 118.

Abbot of Melrose; there, some forfeited estates would come their way—by what means we shall perhaps never know. For instance, although Sir Walter Scott and all the Scott tribe were mixed up in the Earl of Bothwell's mad rebellion, Scott is "graciously pardoned," and is granted Bothwell—his fellow conspirator's—forfeited estates, consisting of the lordship and barony of Hailes and properties in Haddington, Berwick, Selkirk, Dumfries, the lands and lordship of all Liddesdale and the Castle of Hermitage.

The Buccleughs, already growing rapidly in prosperity, do not seem to have been more bloodthirsty than their neighbours, but the Sir Walter Scott, who was head of the House about the end of the 16th century, was accused of burning "innocent creatures within their houses." It would appear that the lands and lordship of Dalkeith were honestly purchased for 480,000 merks; but Sir George Douglas leaves us in no doubt whatever that though part of the extensive lands of the Abbey of Melrose were purchased early in the 18th century, "a portion of them" had previously "been acquired." "The lands of Melrose Abbey were seized," says Sir George, in his admirably written history of the Counties of Roxburgh, Selkirk, and Peebles (p.295), "by the lords of the reformed party in 1559," and as Buccleugh obtained share of the plunder, we may take it he was zealous for the Reformation.

The story of how the family attained ducal honours is worth telling if only to shatter the common prejudice that there is something inherently valorous in the history of every nobleman who is referred to as "His Grace." In 1651 Francis of Buccleugh died, leaving two daughters, Mary and Anna, Mary the elder being only four years of age. No sooner had this child succeeded to the vast Buccleugh estates than she became legitimate prey in the nobility marriage market; and finally in a mass of intrigue she was, when only eleven years of age, married to the Earl of Tarras. The child, however, was worn and faded by the unhappiness entailed through her great possessions, and although Charles II was invited to use his divine and miraculous powers of healing upon her—as a matter of fact he "touched her for the *cruels*"—she pined away and died. Her sister Anna, who succeeded to the estates, now became legitimate prey for Court vultures; but the Merry Monarch warded them off, for he had many illegitimate sons of his own, and here was a prosperous position for one of them. The youth selected for the Buccleugh dominions was the offspring of King Charles' liaison with Lucy Walters or Barlow, and had already been created the Duke of Monmouth. The young heiress was taken to London and married to the boy Duke in the King's private bedchamber, with much the same concern for the tastes and desires of the young pair as if they had been prize poultry or selected rabbits. Immediately the children were married, the King "created" the boy husband "Duke of Buccleugh," and by this title the descendants of the marriage have since demanded and obtained the reverence and homage of all "loyal" Scotsmen. This compulsory marriage was naturally a very unhappy one, and I do not wonder that the Duke of Buccleugh contracted an intimacy with another lady whom he is said to have regarded as his wife in the sight of heaven.

After the union of the Crowns in 1603, King James set himself the task of clearing out the Armstrongs, the "broken men" who infested—military vidette fashion—the debateable lands.

The Armstrongs were ruthlessly cleared out, and never rallied from the cruel "visitation"; indeed from this time they disappear from prominence in the Border country, their lands mostly passing into the omnivorous maw of the Buccleughs. The Scotts have also increased their prosperity by one or two lucky marriages, the Queensberry estates and considerable Montagu property being thus acquired. Of course the origin of much of this Queensberry property is quite as illicit as anything now in the hands of the Buccleughs. Take this as specimen:–

> "It appears from other documents that sundry houses
> in the West Port of Edinburgh, and certain lands in
> the Parish of Cramond, had been gifted to the Cross
> Church of Peebles. All the above sources of income

appear to have been conferred on William, Earl of March, second son of the Duke of Queensberry, at the periods of the Revolution of 1688 and of the Union in 1707, together with 50 acres of rich glebe land lying in the vicinity of the church—only four acres being reserved for the minister of the Parish of Peebles."*

That is to say, Queensberry robbed the church, and the stolen land is to-day held by his descendant, the Duke of Buccleugh. I do not know what precise amount of plunder the Buccleughs succeeded in obtaining from the public purse when they were bought off at the abolition of hereditable jurisdictions in 1747; but they managed to secure £400 for the loss of their hereditary jurisdiction "rights" in Hawick† and the Duke of Queensberry surpassed himself when he demanded £4000 for surrendering the perpetual Sheriffship of Peebles. The Exchequer latterly paid him £3418 4/5, and we may be sure that Queensberry would allow no discount for cash. The four shillings and fivepence would be accepted. Some of the Queensberrys led notoriously dissolute lives. Of the Queensberry who was First Commissioner of the Scots Treasury in Queen Anne's time, Lord Dartmouth says, "He was universally allowed to be very dexterous" at the accumulation of riches. Bishop Burnett says of him, "He engrossed all things to himself, and was a very covetous man." Lord Seafield says, "The whole revenue of Scotland could not satisfy his demands, and he left the rest of the company to shift for themselves."

In more recent years the Buccleughs have not drawn any public attention by fresh attempts to quarter themselves on the public purse or by the pilfering of lands. Possibly the result of the last attempt of the kind (made in the year 1863) on the people of Sanquhar has been a salutary lesson to Dalkeith Palace.

About the year 1860 the then Duke of Buccleugh made a

---

* Statistical Account of Scotland, Vol 3, Sect. Peebles, p. 7
† Ibid, Vol. 3 Sect. Roxburgh, p. 387.

claim on the town of Sanquhar for "arrears of stipend and interest" due to him as "Titular"—some old feudal nonsense or other that gave him legal entry to the public funds. To this piece of audacious impertinence, the Town Council of Sanquhar boldly replied by a counter-action for "arrears of feu-rents for lands held by His Grace from the Town." Of course His Grace was furious, but the Court of Session upheld the town's claim, and decreed that Sanquhar was entitled to receive from the Duke £1156 1/8; while the Duke, though he won his case for "stipend and interest," only got £110 5/11; thus losing well over £1000 through his insatiate greed.§

---

§ "The History of Sanquhar "—J. Brown, p. 236.

THE SUTHERLANDS.

"All the people of spirit and enterprise leave the country; for everything done in Sutherland must be under the eye of the factor, and in the interest of Dunrobin. It is the Duke! the Duke! the Duke! There is no room for enterprise or any independent spirit; a man cannot trench a rood of ground without asking leave of the ground officer or some such official . . . There are, so far as I can make out, between 7000 and 8000 people in the Reay Country. . . and all that population . . . have only somewhere about one-thirteenth part of the Reay Country allowed to them— 7000 or 8000 people—and the rest is under sheep, under deer, under hares, under rabbits, and under grouse and other unprofitable occupants of the soil. . . We are in fact under an absolute despotism."

—*Rev. Jas. Cumming, Free Church Minster,*
Melness, 1884.
Evidence before the Crofters' Commission.

"I find their (the people's) liberty is interfered with in connection with the election of School Boards, Poor Boards, and Road Trustees, and so on."

Rev. D. Mackenzie, Free Church Minister, Farr.
Evidence before the Crofters' Commission, 1883.

"Under the old Celtic tenure the chiefs were not owners of the soil. The land was really the property of the clan. After the rebellion of 1745 all this was changed. The chiefs were made owners of the land, the ancient rights of the people being entirely ignored."   —*Maclaren*

IN a previous article of this series dealing with the house of Atholl, I said that the family of Stewart Murray was founded by the land pirate Hugo Freskyn or Freskin. And now in searching the records of the noble Family of Sutherland, I find that its blue blood comes from the same gentleman. I begin to be interested in this Hugo. He floats about in the dawn of the land history of Scotland, murdering, massacring, laying waste and settling the conquered lands on his offspring. The historians know little of his origin, but Chalmers in "Caledonia" declares that he was a Fleming. As a free-booter he was a decided success, and when the "Morrayes, who had been since A.D. 63 expelled from Germany" displeased the King of Scotland about the beginning of the 13th. Century, the amiable Freskin was sent north to administer Freskin justice, which form of justice appears to put the famous Jeddart variety to shame. After he had rooted out the "Morrayes," Freskin settled a large estate in Sutherlandshire (confirmed by Royal "Grant") on one of his sons—and so began the Noble house of Sutherland. Rooted in theft (for as every legal authority admits, the clan, or children of the soil were the only proprietors), casting every canon of morality to the winds, this family has waxed fat on misery, and, finally, less than 100 years ago, perpetrated such abominable cruelties on the tenantry as aroused the disgust and anger of the whole civilised world.

In the Landowners' Return (1874) the Duke and Duchess of Sutherland are credited with land property as follows:–

	Acres.	*Rental.*
Ross-shire	149,999	£12,002
Sutherlandshire	1,176,454	56,937

To which add:–

Salop	17,495	40,418
Stafford	12,744	29,987
York	1,853	2,323
Totals	1,358,545	£141,667

From all of which it will appear that this "noble" family is doing very well under the present system, and is quite of the same opinion as the Tory working man, that our land laws are as perfect as it is possible to make them, and that any interference with the Sutherland family's "right" to levy an annual tax of £69,000 on the impoverished Highlander would be as terrible and detestable as cannibalism or *lese majeste.*

Those of our noble families who are sufficiently brazen-faced and unashamed as have their histories written, have usually employed some greasy sophist well skilled in making the worse appear the better reason, to make the record palatable; and the Sutherlands are no exception to the rule. The history of the Sutherland Family, written by Sir William Fraser, in three immense volumes, is, in so far as it deals with matters of vital moment, simply a travesty of history, and has snobbish humbug stamped on nearly every page of it.

Hearken to his conclusion of the whole matter!

". . . The Duke of Sutherland has vied with his pred-
ecessors in taking measures for the welfare of the
people." *

"Welfare of the people"! The blatant impertinence of it! Why, out of Sir William's own volumes I could convict the Sutherlands of every crime and infamy I ever heard of—and some that were entirely unknown to me, till I read his pages.

The welfare of the people! Let us go back the records for a moment or two!

Here in Sir William's history we read of cruel murders and blatant thievings. John the Eighth Earl of Sutherland is perpetually being sued by other proprietors who declare that he "wrongfully occupies" their lands and withholds "the rents of these lands and

---

* Vol. I., p. 37.

the fishings attached." In 1494 he was accused and convicted of stealing the Castle of Skelbo and "two children of John Murray." Two sons of his illegitimate brother Thomas, he "orders to be killed." The next Earl of Sutherland is described by Sir Robert Gordon, the earliest historian of the family, as "weak of judgement, deprived of naturall witt and understanding, being able to governe neither himself nor others." This weakling Duke was slain and his head hoisted on Dunrobin Castle by his brother-in-law, who usurped the "rights." His idea of "rights" may be guessed when we find him shortly afterwards being sued at law by the Countess of Huntly for "carrying off the lands of Dawane and much property, including feather beds, bolsters, and other furnishings." In 1532 he was convicted of stealing tiends from the Dean of Dunbar and the parson of Rathven.

The Countess of Sutherland (circa 1560) appears to have been a very marriageable lady, and had survived five husbands. At the time of the Reformation struggles, the Sutherlands blew neither hot nor cold, or rather they blew both ways, and were always friends with the winning party. But my lord of Sutherland overstepped himself, and being concerned in some nefarious business for the capture of Queen Mary, was promptly banished to France. Later he returned to Sutherlandshire, and appears to have abandoned the risky calling of high politics for the more lucrative occupation of adding church lands to his estates. One of these acquisitions was Scrabster and Scrabster Castle, and it was at this time (1561) that "thirling" began. All tenants, husbandmen, and inhabitants were ordered to carry all corns to the Duke's mills and pay "righteous multures" there. Thirling was monopoly milling with the Duke charging monopoly prices. This Duke was poisoned, and I do not read of any extraordinary lamentations on his demise. If the present Duke is animated by any such kindly feelings for the welfare of the people as these gentry I have just mentioned, he has an excellent chance of one day dancing at the end of a hangman's rope.

But why go on with such records of pitiful knaveries? Why detail the "successful" marriages and the adding of field to field and hillside to hillside until there was no room—are not these things the commonplaces in the history of all landlordism?

Sutherlandshire has been slowly impoverished by rent-drawing and the stupidities consequent on private ownership of the soil, but the climax was reached at the beginning of last century, when the Duke saw "money" in the development of the vast estates.

About that time the then Duchess had married a Lord Gower, Marquis of Stafford. He had, as the French say, a dot of his own, and on his arrival in the North, and seeing the immense possibilities that lay before the Highlands if they were properly developed, he proceeded judiciously to make a "corner" in the ownership of Sutherlandshire and Ross-shire by buying out as many of the impoverished petty landlords as he could. In 1829 he bought the whole Reay estates and then he gradually "licked up" Bighouse, Skelbo, Armadale and Strathy, Torboll, Uppat Carrol, Ardross, part of the Kyles of Oykel and the Dornoch Firth, Inverar, the Superiority of the Burgh of Wick, Creich, where only the other day a poor man's house was reported to be burned to the ground by a Sheriff's officer because he, the poor man, was unable to pay his taxes, Langwell, Sandycroft, Teabreck—all were grist to the Sutherland Mill, and the family estates now ran from Dornoch on the east to Cape Wrath on the West.

Then came the new "development," which took several forms, but the one that principally concerns us here is the ruthless, cruel, and murderous manner in which the crofts were burned, and crofters' families huddled, starving, and shivering, to the sea-shore, in order to facilitate the creation of huge sheep runs, of which the Duke had doubtless golden dreams.

Now I am aware that there has been much disputing over parts of the evidence about these Sutherland clearances. I know that Dr. Alfred Russell Wallace had to withdraw and tone down some statements which appeared in the first edition of his work on Land Nationalisation. I have read Mr. Thos. Sellars' elaborate defence of his father, who was the principal Sutherland underling in these horrible clearances, and I know that Sellar himself was acquitted in court of some of the charges made against him; still, there is no explaining away the main charges, and we can well afford to ignore the minor stories which have been disputed or which rest on insufficient evidence. But although Patrick Sellar was given a verdict of "Not Guilty," it is as well to keep on record the fact that the Court was a landlords' Court, that many of the witnesses would be obviously terrorised, and that the principal witness for the prosecution, Sheriff-Substitute M'Kid, had his evidence refused on a technical legal quibble, and that for the noble part he took in this business, he, M'Kid, was forced to resign his position, and leave the North of Scotland, nobody evidently knowing what became of him. When the forces of landlordism were powerful enough to eject from office a Sheriff Substitute, it is small wonder that the witnesses for the prosecution got shaky.

However, we can leave Patrick Sellar; the main facts about the clearances have never successfully been disputed, and they are quite enough for my purpose.

Huge farms were deemed more profitable to the landlord than small crofts; and in several parishes the entire crofting population got notice to "clear out." Crops were standing uncut in many cases; the houses had all been built by the tenants or their ancestors; and they, the tenants, had nowhere else to go. It is true many of the crofters were offered "allotments" on the barren seashore; it is true they were given the privilege of gathering whelks for food, and of fishing in the rough seas of the outer main if they could lay their hands on sufficient money to purchase a boat. Still they had no money for boat purchasings; they had no desire to leave their almost ripe crops at a landlord's whim, and betake themselves away from the family croft on the ancestral strath to make corn grow on sea-shingle! They thought their homes were their own, and that, having improved it, they had some rights in the soil and in the growing crops. Alas! Down swept the Apaches from Dunrobin Castle; whole parishes were "cleared," roof trees pulled down, and the little crofts, and frequently the miserable furniture, committed to the flames, with the women and children weeping by the roadside. In one or two cases the pillagers did not even trouble to remove sick persons before setting fire to the thatch; women almost in childbirth were thrown on the roadside; ruin— red, hopeless ruin—everywhere, cruelties and savageries almost unmentionable and unbelievable, clouds of smoke filling the valleys, and the peasantry that had been a country's pride hunted, ragged and homeless, to a barren coast!

Let us take the evidence of James Macdonald, retired revenue officer, aged 81, before the Crofters' Commission in 1884.* I select this old man because he was a Tory, and talked during his evidence about the "generous nobleman." His evidence was not likely to be biased in favour of the Crofters. Yet he called the "clearances" in the Parish of Clyne "distressing," and they "left a painful impression on his mind."

> The expelled people "would morally, mentally, and physically compare favourably side by side with any other peasantry in the world . . . I beg to assure your honours that I have seen the atmosphere in Clyne and for many miles around, filled with the smoke which arose from the burning cottages from which their inmates had been forcibly ejected, in the Straths of Kildonan, Brora, Fleet, etc. Other cottages I have seen in the act of being demolished—levelled with the ground; and I *have seen the people who had occupied them for days without shelter, huddled together at dykesides, and roadsides and on the beach,* waiting the arrival of ships to carry them across the Atlantic, or wherever they were forced to go. I have a distinct recollection of *seeing a notice that was issued simultaneously with those proceedings, posted upon the door of the Parish Church, intimating that any person who was known to have given shelter to, or to have harboured any of the evicted people,*

---

* Page 3222, Vol. 4.

*would, in turn, without any warning, be summarily ejected
from his or her house, and be compelled to leave the country;* and this harsh decree applied irrespective of any
ties of relationship whatsoever."

The first of these "clearances" began in Ross-shire about 1800, but
owing to the frantic opposition of the tenantry was abandoned. Then
in 1807 about 90 families were "removed" from the parishes of Farr
and Larg. Through having to sleep in the open-air some of the
weaker among the dispossessed were hurried off to an early grave.

Scarcely had the echoes of the Farr and Larg scandal died
away ere "several hundred families" were cleared out of the parishes
of Dornoch, Rogart, Loth, Clyne, and Golspie. These removals
took place in 1809. Then in 1811 preparations were carefully made
for an extensive "rooting out," and the actors in the bogus
"Sutherlandshire Rebellion" were ready with the dodges which
were successfully copied by the Uitlanders in South Africa. One
worthy, Reid by name, a manager on a Kildonan sheep farm,
declared that he had been hunted for his life by the natives and put
in bodily fear. Then special constables were sworn in, the cannon
at Dunrobin Castle were trimmed and charged, the Riot Act was
read, a few wondering natives were clapped in Dornoch Jail,
evidently to add a touch of realism to the comedy, and a regiment
of Irish was sent by forced marches from Fort George, with artillery
and cart loads of ammunition to suppress the Rebellion!

The soldiers, strangely enough, found no rebellion to
suppress, but their appearance was all that had been desired, and
with the might of the British Empire behind the "removers," the
clearance scheme proceeded apace.

In May, 1814, the whole parishes of Farr and Kildonan were
completely cleared of any who had been overlooked in previous
clearances. An eyewitness of this particular removal says:–

"Many deaths ensued from alarm, from fatigue, and
cold; the people being instantly deprived of shelter

and left to the mercy of the elements. Some old men took to the woods and precipices, wandering about in a state approaching to, or of absolute insanity, and several of them in this condition lived only a few days. Pregnant women were taken with premature labour, and several children did not long survive their sufferings. . . Donald Macbeth, an infirm and bed-ridden old man, had the house unroofed over him and was, in that state, exposed to the wind till death put an end to his sufferings. I was present at the pulling down and burning of the house of William Chisholm, Badinloskin, in which was lying his wife's mother, an old bed-ridden woman of near 100 years of age. The factor on his arrival was told of this, but he replied— 'Damn her, the old witch, she has lived too long; let her burn.' Fire was immediately set to the house and the blankets in which she was carried were in flames before she could be got out. She was placed in a little shed, and it was with great difficulty they were prevented from firing it also. The old woman's daughter arrived when the house was on fire, and assisted the neighbours in removing her mother out of the flames and smoke, presenting a picture of horror which I shall never forget, but cannot attempt to describe. She died within five days."†

The people were now in desperation. Even Mr. Loch in his elaborate defence of the Sutherlands admits (p. 76) that the people lived on cockles they picked up on the seashore, and on broth made from nettles, and as (although no one to this day accurately knows the number of evicted people in these clearances) some 2000 people had been evicted in Kildonan, and some 2000 in Strathnaver, one can better imagine than describe the state of Sutherlandshire in the year of grace 1820.

It has been offered in defence of the Sutherlands that £3000 was "given in loan to these poor people who lost their cattle." This statement has been vehemently denied by the Crofters, who declare

† Donald M'Leod— "Gloomy Memories of the Highlands," p. 9.

that they never saw a penny of that money; and as for the much-belauded "charity" given to the dispossessed in the shape of meal, no greater fraud was ever practised on the Highlanders. The people had been robbed of their all, and driven from their homes; and they were given meal in charity! Charity, forsooth! *The charity was charged for at the next Martinmas term at the rate of 50/ per boll*, and payment was rigorously extorted, those having cattle being obliged to give them up to liquidate the debt! But let us come down to a later date, for in the case of the Sutherlands we have distinct and reliable evidence of what the landlord was doing about the time of the Crofters' Commission, that is, about the year 1883.

Before that Commission, the Rev. James Cumming, minister of Melness, gave evidence startling enough even by itself to cause a radical sweeping away of the territorial nobility landowning business. He had been minister in Melness for 22 years, and he declared that the people were emigrating because they had no room to live. One huge sheep farm at their very doors swallowed up about 70,000 acres. The people were refused leases, even of the houses they themselves had built. They were subject to "petty molestation" from the estate agents; they were under estate laws which frequently went against both letter and spirit of existing Imperial land laws; they were subject to fines which ultimately found their way into a fixed charge in the rent.*

> "If a man receives a lodger into his house—his son-in-law or his daughter-in-law—he is subject to a fine, and that fine, in some instances, if not all, gradually finds its way into the rent and becomes an increase of rent."

Another witness representing the Crofters of Leadnagullen handed in a written statement, which included the following:–

> "At the time of the Strathnaver evictions, the land allotted to us was wholly unreclaimed. It was valued

---

* Crofters' Commission Evidence. Vol. II,. p. 1594

> at £2 10/, and after years of industry on our part,
> without any aid from the proprietor, our labours were
> rewarded by raising the rental to above £20."†

Another witness told of an old woman who was to be evicted because she had housed her destitute brother-in-law, who was "at enmity" with the factor, and the ground officer was sent

> "Round the district forbidding the people upon pain
> of eviction to give her shelter in their houses."

And—here is the end of the story:–

> "The thing preyed upon her mind so much that when
> the day of final eviction came, she died about twelve
> o'clock, broken-hearted, the ground officer and sheriff
> officer being then within half a mile of her house on
> their way to evict her."

I could tell of parishes where, according to the local clergymen, there were no marriages, nor could there be any, for no house or land could be got, for:–

> "it is against the estate law, and though it is a hard-
> ship that young people cannot marry, yet the law of
> the estate is good that they should not marry without
> a house and lands, and no houses or land can be got."§

But these and similar tyrannies and follies are not peculiar to the Sutherlands; they are the common blots on the scutcheons of our landed gentry, but when the day of reckoning comes—and by all portents it will not be long—let it may be remembered that the people who suffered the wrongs patiently were as much to blame for the shame as were the landlord tyrants themselves.

---

† Page 1611, Ibid.
§ Rev. J. Ross (Durness)—Statement at Kinlochbervie.

THE GORDONS

AND THEIR ROYAL DESCENT!

"The extent to which the Church, even in the fifteenth century, endeavoured to hold in check the oppressors of the poor and weak is manifest in the confessional books of the period. Not only usurers and false traders were denounced, but princes and magistrates boldly reproved."

—Karl Pearson,
"The Chances of Death," Vol. II., p. 252.

"There were few among the greater lairds who had not participated in the spoils of the Church."
W. Watt, County History Series, "Aberdeenshire," p. 173.

"The Gordon, the gool, and the hoodie-craw
Were the three worst evils Moray ever saw."

THE Gordons were a nest of public robbers whose base of operations was the North-East of Scotland. For centuries they harried the commons, plundered the Church, stole everything they could lay their hands on, and kept the north in a perpetual uproar and bloodshed with their forays and feuds. When the chief pirate emerged from his fastness at Strathbogie, he swept everything bare; and although to-day the family fortunes have fallen, and there are police in the land to keep these human vultures and assassins somewhat in order, their "noble" descendants still fatten on public property; they still draw rents from stolen lands; they still oppress the poor.

There are many septs and branches of the Gordons holding land; and in Scotland alone in the year 1874 their acreage and spoil was officially returned as follows:–

Aberdeenshire—	*Acres.*	*Gross Annual Rental.*
Gordon of Avochie	850	675
Gordon of Ellon	6,092	3,652
Gordon of Ellon	5,556	6,194
Gordon of Newton	3,369	2,989
Gordon of Rayne	830	999
Gordon of Kildrummy	13,427	6,876
Gordon of Kincardine	1,716	1,047
Gordon of Udny	235	254
Sir H. P. Gordon of Niton	6,709	3,438
Gordon of Hallhd. and Esslemont	4,962	4,502
Gordon of Manar	2,260	2,114
Gordon of Craig	3,333	1,139
Gordon of Cairness	4,100	3,476
Gordon of Cluny	20,395	13,713
Gordon of Craigmyle	3,200	1,884
Gordon of Buthlaw	1,124	1,287
Gordon of Dunnydear	727	616
Colonel Gordon of Fyvie	11,700	8,741
Gordon of Glasgoforest	1,970	2,144
Gordon of Sandfordhill	399	370
Marquis of Huntly	80,000	11,215
Duke of Richmond and Gordon	69,660	24,747
Earl of Aberdeen	63,422	40,765
Banffshire—		
Gordon of Avochie	2,171	1,528
Gordon of Cluny	2,734	2,724
Gordon of Cairnfield	3,175	1,362
Gordon of Letterfourie	1,720	1,982
Duke of Richmond and Gordon	159,952	23,841
Berwickshire—		
Gordon of Belchester	484	1,145
Dumfries—		
Gordon of Letterfourie	151	300
Edinburgh—		
Gordon of Cluny	701	2,116

Elginshire—		
Duke of Richmond and Gordon	12,271	10,618
Forfarshire—		
Lord Hallyburton	5,119	7,048
Inverness-shire—		
Gordon of Cluny	84,404	8,954
Duke of Richmond and Gordon	27,409	1,182
Kincardineshire—		
Gordon of Fyvie	1,340	906
Kirkcudbright—		
Gordon of Letterfourie	460	437
Gordon of Earlston	765	1,179
Nairnshire—		
Gordon of Cluny	3,635	2,536
Perthshire—		
Admiral Hallyburton	361	181
	612,888	£210,876

I confess that the stupendous iniquity bound up in what these figures really mean moves me to amazement at my countrymen. Here, fattening like slugs on a cabbage, living idly on the toil and moil and worry of others, here, if you please, a small but merry family party of Gordons clutching lands *one and a half times the size of Banffshire!* How can I impress my readers with the magnitude of the plunder? Two hundred and ten thousand pounds per annum! Tenpence halfpenny per pound of the whole assessable rental of the City of Glasgow, handed over to a handful of idle "work-shys" and "spongers"— handed over every year by the hard-headed shrewd, canny, bawbee-saving Scot, handed over without a murmur, handed over with pleasure and amid the singing of "Rule Britannia" and cries of "Protect our goods against the foreigner!"

Nor does my table tell the full tale of the tribute these parasites exact from us. Down in Kirkcudbrightshire there is a small nest of Gordons whom I cannot connect with the main stock; and of course there is much land spoil raped from the simple English across the Border, the Duke of Richmond and Gordon, for instance, owning over 17,000 valuable acres in Sussex.

Let us see how they got all this land. Did they get it honestly, or did they acquire it by such methods that we are merely qualifying ourselves for the mocking scorn of future generations by allowing them to retain it any longer?

We shall enquire into the history of the Duke of Richmond and Gordon, who is the largest landholder of the tribe, and then we shall give a short summary of the history of the whole Gordon family.

The first Duke of Richmond makes his appearance in unsavoury circumstances. Louise Renee de Perrencourt de Querouaille was a French spy sent over to the English Court by Louis XIV in the hey-day of the Merry Monarch, King Charles II. The spy's best method of procuring information in those times was by attaching himself or herself to Court, and to the King's party if possible. But Louise went one better—or worse. She became, to put it bluntly, a Court harlot, and succeeded in attaching herself to the dissolute King. The Queen was living, and Bishop Burnet in his "History" tells us of the scandal caused by King Charles' visits to the French adultress; but we may safely skip the prurient details of the Royal *liaison*, which are given in some of the records of the time. Charles got infatuated with Louise. He created her Duchess of Portsmouth, Countess of Farcham, and Baroness Petersfield—and she evidently looked after French interests so well that King Louis created her Duchess d'Aubigny, and handed over to her the d'Aubigny estates. Then a child was born, King Charles being proclaimed its father; and the King, who was anything but mean—with other people's property—created his offspring at the age of three, Duke of Richmond and Lennox, giving him at the same time the vast Lennox estates in Scotland and the Castle of Richmond in Yorkshire. He also granted him Charlton Forest. Still the open-handed Monarch did not stop there. He was determined, like a wise father, to see to the future of his dozen illegitimate children, so long, of course, as it could be done at the expense of a long-suffering people. To the young Duke of Richmond he granted for all time coming the "right" to one shilling per chaldron upon all coals shipped on the River Tyne, to be consumed in England! This gigantic robbery went on unchecked till George III's time, when a landlord Parliament bought the ducal cormorant off for an annuity of £19,000. At the age of nine, the young Duke, we are told, was given the Order of the Garter, and we know that he later on cut a somewhat conspicuous figure as a vested interest defender in Parliament. Says Mr. Howard Evans*:–

> "It ought to be mentioned that the only time when the first Duke of Richmond distinguished himself in Parliament was in the angry debate on the Resumption Bill of 1700. Down to the time of Henry VIII Acts of Resumption, restoring to the Crown lands which had been lavishly granted away, were passed in almost every reign, and the enormous alienations of Crown property which had taken place in the reigns of Charles II and William III led to a determined effort on the part of the House of Commons to pass another Act of Resumption, which was resisted by the Peers, many of whom were, of course, directly interested in the matter. The cry was that the nation was being ruined by the three B.s' – Bishops, Bastards, and Beggars. The Resumption Bill of 1700 only applied to Dutch Beggars; but Royal Bastards became fearful that they might be next attacked, and the first name that appears on the protest of certain lords to the Bill in question is that of the Duke of Richmond."

The second Duke, though his grandfather was a Stuart, distinguished himself in history as a Lord of the Bedchamber to George II, and as High Constable of England at his Coronation ceremony. He inherited the d'Aubigny estates from his grandmother; but the French Revolution soon put a stop to plunder in that quarter. The third Duke, at the Coronation of George III, rendered valuable public service—"carrying the sceptre with the dove." He was somewhat of a Radical, however, and not only

* "Our Old Nobility," p. 110.

proposed manhood suffrage, but Annual Parliaments, and he seems to have been one of the few lords of his generation who saw the folly of the British position during the American War of Independence. The fifth Duke, in 1783, succeeded to the Gordon estates in Scotland through a lucky family marriage, and in the House of Lords was noted for his vigorous support of the landed interest during the struggle to repeal the Corn Laws. From an extremely, indeed, ludicrously sycophantic work entitled "Records and Reminiscences of Goodwood and the Dukes of Richmond," I learn that the late Duke was a very generous landlord, and that he allowed abatements of rents to the amount of £88,000 between the years of 1879 and 1894. That is to say, he allowed 15 months' rent in 15 years, but nothing is said about the other 13 years and 9 months, during which he drew some £60,000 per annum from Scotland. His family motto is "En la Rose Je Fleuris," but I'm afraid it's not altogether on the Rose he flourishes. There's something to be said for the stupidity of the British people.

In a previous paper I dealt with the Gordons of Barra and their brutal treatment of the poor Islanders. Let us now roughly go over the salient features of the history of the main Gordon stock.

It appears that the first Gordon in Scotland was a Fleming, who accompanied King Malcolm III, and who for his dutiful services as a mercenary warrior was allotted some lands in Berwickshire. He settled himself down on the borders as a capable freebooter, and after a long and prosperous career, was succeeded by his son, who, we are told, "died fighting for his lands." † Of their descendants, to the time of Robert the Bruce, there is little noteworthy to relate, but after Bruce had driven out the English, the Gordon fortunes were augmented "bountifully "—most likely from the public purse. In the time of King Robert I, an illegitimate son of Sir John Gordon managed to secure the forfeited lands of

---

† "History of the House of Gordon," C. A. Gordon, p. 7.

the Cummings of Strathbogie, in grant from the King. In 1358 the Gordons wheedled a charter to the lands and forest of Enzie and Boyne from King David. Sir Adam, the seventh Gordon chief, being slain at Hambledonhill, in 1403, and leaving behind him one legitimate daughter and two illegitimate sons, the family split up into sections. The daughter married Sir William Seaton, who assumed the title of Gordon. By 1457 they had added many fields to their estates, and were the greatest power in the North of Scotland. Hungry retainers of little twopenny lords were seduced away and took the name of Gordon and the oath of vassalage in return for a "bow of meal." By the year 1457 the Earl of Huntly (as the Gordon chief was now named) owned the lands of Strathbogie, Aboyne, Glentaner, Glenmuick, the lordship of Badenoch, and the Enzie, in addition to the original lands in Berwickshire. The second Earl, we are told,§ "added the lands of Schivas, in Buchan and Boyne, and Netherdale, in Banffshire." He did not purchase them, you will observe, he merely "added" them; and so strong a power does he appear to have been in the North that not only were the burghers of Aberdeen in constant fear of him, but he contrived to marry himself to the Princess Annabella, daughter of James I. The third Earl, "added Strathaven or Strathdoun, in Banffshire, and the Brae of Lochaber, in Inverness." ¶ That significant word "added" again! The fourth Earl, not satisfied with his possessions, managed to induce King James V to give him the lordship of Braemar, Strathdee, and Cromar, except Migvie. He was "Cock of the North" and maintained a lavish expenditure. His "Court" was comparable only with that of England or France, and a contemporary visitor to his board tells us that "his cheer is marvellous great."

About this time the Church had still vast lands and endowments; indeed, Mr. Watt goes so far as to say that it owned *"probably half the wealth"* in Scotland! There are, however, other

§ "Aberdeen and Banff," W. Watt. P. 88.
¶ Ibid, p. 142.

authorities who put the proportion at one-third. This half or this third, whichever it was, clearly became a standing temptation to the nobles of the period, and Huntly was by no means the least of the robbers who plundered the Church. A Gordon was foisted into the episcopal office at Aberdeen,

> "And on the eve of the Reformation feus and leases
> of the Church lands were granted in large numbers
> and on easy terms to the family connections of the
> Gordon interest."**

After that, of course, Gordon—we know not what he was before—became a zealous and conspicuous opponent of the Reformation of the Church. A combination of the nobles of the Protestant party managed to slay him, and to scatter his forces at the Battle of Corrichie.

The next Earl carried matters with a high hand, beheading and hanging all who would not obey him; and one of his relatives, Gordon of Auchindoun, out with a pack of midnight freebooters and thieves, in the year 1591, committed an act of atrocity and barbarism that shocked even the reckless robbers and cutpurses of the time. The Gordons had appeared at the house of Forbes of Towie and demanded its surrender. Forbes was from home, but his wife refused to open the door, whereupon the Gordons set the whole place on fire, and roasted everybody—man, woman, and child—in the flames. Remember that this happened almost at the beginning of the seventeenth century! The Gordons, the Keiths, and the Forbes kept the North-East in a perpetual turmoil, and there was a pleasant game practised on the citizens of Aberdeen, by means of which each side of noble thieves in turn accused the citizens of Aberdeen of being in sympathy with their absent enemies. This accusation, of course, was merely a preliminary to a demand for ransom lest some terrible destruction should immediately befall their town. On one occasion the Town Council on behalf of the citizens retorted:–

** Ibid, p. 137.

> "If the noblemen insist to have the said taxation (100,000 merks) they desire a competent time, a month or thereby, to be granted them to remove themselves and their wives and bairns with baggage out of the town, and thereafter let the noblement dispose of the town at their pleasure."††

This shows with accuracy what the burghers of Aberdeen must have suffered from the nobility.

As a general rule the Gordons have been Royalists, Anti-Reformists, Tories, and Reactionaries, though there is a certain daring bravery about their rogueries that somehow contrasts pleasantly with the cunning of the Primroses, the petty deceits of the Stairs, or the meanness of the Duffs. When they stole, they did it on a liberal scale, and were little but glorified highwaymen.

At the present day they are merely a flock of human locusts eating up a large part of the labour of Scotsmen; they are, as landowners, fulfilling no useful function; they are but drones in the hive, dry grass fit for the economic oven.

---

†† Burgh Records of Aberdeen, p. 157.

THE CAMPBELLS OF ARGYLL.

"Now, obviously, the magistrates of the State must be
chosen out of the superior class . . . These are the true
guardians of the State; the remainder are to be called
Auxiliaries. And in order to convince the citizens of
the wisdom and justice of this order of things, we must
tell them a story, to the effect that they were all originally fashioned in the bowels of the earth, their common mother; and that it pleased the gods to mix gold
in the composition of some of them, silver in that of
others, iron and copper in that of others."

Plato's "Republic," Davies & Vaughan, p. 17.

"God's malison and mine I give to them that know of
this gear and restore it not."

"As time passed, and the prospects of the division of
the Church lands approached, they (the Nobles) grew
firmer in their adherence to the principles of the Reformation."

Macintosh's "Scotland," p. 107.
Story of the Nation Series.

THE family of Campbell is now split up into three powerful divisions,
the Campbells of Argyll, the Campbells of Breadalbane, and the
Campbells of Cawdor. Together, they have contrived to accumulate
about $1\frac{1}{4}$ million acres of Scotland, which brings them an annual
rental of over £250,000; but for purposes of historical analysis
(though they are all descended from the one man) it is advisable to
treat each division separately.

It has been declared that there are no facts in Ireland, and the same may be truthfully said of the early history of the Campbells of Argyll. The Argylls, so far as I can discover, have published no official family history; most of the church records have been stolen or destroyed, and writer after writer in the Statistical Account of Scotland bewails the absence of authentic information on the early history of Argyllshire. The earliest Campbell we have record of was one Gillespie Campbell, who, some eight centuries ago, acquired by marriage with the daughter of the then Treasurer of Scotland, the lordship of Lochow. The Argyll branch had acquired by the year 1874 lands and land rents as follows:–

Ayrshire—	*Acres.*	*Gross Ann. Rental.*
Countess of Loudon	18,638	£15,286
Countess of Loudon (Mines)	–	2,259
Dumbartonshire—		
Duke of Argyll	6,799	5,170
Campbell of Cameseskan	2,124	2,419
Campbell of Succoth	2,395	6,254
Edinburghshire—		
Campbell of Succoth	233	1,649
Inverness—		
Campbell of Fassifern	74,000	4,827
Stirlingshire—		
Campbell of Succoth	926	1,567
Campbell of Balquhan	5,679	3,185
Argyllshire—		
Campbell of Auchendarroch	7,017	1,599
Campbell of Monzie	13,000	1,402
Campbell of Glendaruel	14,032	2,361
Campbell of Highwood	4,067	983
Campbell of Stonefield	35,186	5,813
Campbell of Tighnabruaich	9,521	1,933
Campbell of Barbreck	10,369	2,461
Sir Donald Campbell of Dunstaffnage	3,000	915
Campbell of Baleveolan, Appin	3,500	784
Campbell of Strachur	24,593	3,286
Campbell of Ardlarach	500	135

Campbell of Lochnell	39,000	6,801
Campbell of Colintraive	19,736	2,245
Campbell of Asknish	8,838	1,682
Campbell of Aros	46,000	3,691
Sir George Campbell of Cumlodden	6,787	1,209
Campbell of New Inverawe	900	270
Campbell of Ardrishaig	11,810	2,977
Campbell of Kilberry	20,000	2,173
Campbell of Drimnamuchloch	2,880	660
Campbell of Lerags	1,500	485
Campbell of Shervain	10,841	1,756
Campbell of Ardpatrick	1,250	384
Campbells of Ardow, Auchinbreck, and Ballochyle	6,253	1,085
Lieut.-Colonel Campbell	11,404	1,841
Campbell of Jura	55,000	2,914
Campbells of Sonochan and Ballinaby	2,466	588
Campbells of Ormsary	11,000	1,480
Campbells of Melfort, Fassifern, Ormidale, Dunmore, and Bragleen	22,880	2,708
Duke of Argyll	168,315	45,672
	682,439	£144,548

The Knights of Lochow were stout champions of Robert the Bruce, and on his success rose to position and plenty; but, while they appear to have got a grant of some land at Kilmun about the year 1343, they do not figure prominently in land history until the power of the Macdonalds had grown so strong that it became a matter of vital policy on the part of the Scottish Crown to assist and subsidise the Campbells in the harrowing and weakening of the Macdonalds.

The Macdonalds claimed descent from Somerled, Lord of Kintyre, who was, according to the senachies or bards, a direct descendant of one of the Irish-Scoto kings who had been seated on the Pictish throne.

The Campbells made no mistakes in the treatment they—

with the Crown behind them—meted out to the Macdonalds, and when after generations of savage brutality and cruelty on both sides, the Macdonalds were forced to flee to Ireland in 1613, the Campbell Chief stepped into the ownership of all Kintyre.

Precisely by what means the Campbells obtained all the vast tracts of territory they held in the 16th and 17th centuries, we may never exactly know; but here and there, through the mists, we catch a glimpse of savage butchery, cold, calculating cruelty, and merciless greed; we hear snatches from unseen and nameless senachies of wild clans butchered to the last man, we hear the cries of the dispossessed; and in stray documents that have survived the obliterations of time, unknown scribes have given indications of the ferocity, the theft, the murdering, and the stamping out of the smaller clans which have all contributed to the founding of the glory of the House of Campbell. Let me, as an indication of these things, give the history of how the Campbells acquired Ardnamurchan and Sunart.

For a long period before the year 1519 Ardnamurchan and Sunart had been held by the M'Ians, who were great favourites with the Stuarts. On the death of James IV the neighbouring proprietors united against the M'Ian, scattered his forces, and slew him and his sons.

Thereupon the estates devolved upon his granddaughter, Moriada, who was "induced" (the Statistical Account says "It is not known for what cause") to resign her patrimony to the Earl of Argyll. This "gift" was, however, contrary both to the Crown Charters on which the lands were held, and to the Gaelic rules of succession, and so 60 years afterwards the heirs of M'Ian recovered possession. In 1596, while the Clan M'Ian was weakened by family quarrels:–

> "The occasion was seized by Argyll to enforce the not forgotten deed of Moriada . . . The title deeds of the heir of Macvic Eoin (M'Ian) came into the possession of Argyll, tradition says, by his having found them with a burgess of Edinburgh, with whom M'Ian left

them as pledge for a debt incurred in educating his son. In 1602 M'Ian became, by a special agreement, vassal of Argyll, and in a few years it would seem that the superior acquired the rights of actual proprietor. The clan were, as might be expected from their ignorance of feudal rights, refractory. Mr. Donald Campbell of Baslerick, afterwards Sir Donald Campbell of Ardnamurchan, a man of uncommon depth of policy and inflexible resolution, was appointed by Argyll, his commissioner, to reduce them to obedience. Campbell, by a combination of cruelty and insult, soon goaded the clansmen to violence, and in 1624, twenty-two years after the contract with Argyll, we find them driven to absolute desperation, and above 100 of their fighting men, in an English ship which they had seized, carrying terror as pirates through the North-Western Coasts of Scotland. The close of their history followed speedily. . . They were either extirpated by the sword, or driven into exile with an unsparing severity, which left not even their name behind. Sir Donald Campbell became proprietor of Ardnamurchan, and the race of Ian were no more seen in the Highland Clans."*

As with Ardnamurchan and Sunart, so it must have been with much of the other territory grabbed by the Campbells. Tiree and Coll were "acquired" in 1674, after the Macleans of Duart had been scattered and broken; and Iona was "acquired" about the same time.

Previous to finally "acquiring" Iona, the Earl of Argyll with other "Protestant" friends had been busy suppressing "idolatry," which suppression took the form of destroying valuable books, records, buildings, and monuments of great antiquity, that had been left unmolested for ages by the rude barbarians of the outer Isles. The lands of the lords of Lorn were added by marriage.

Of the personalities of the various Campbell chiefs up to the Reformation struggle there is little noteworthy or reliable to relate.

---

* Stat. Account of Scotland. Vol. 7, Argyllshire, p. 138, Article by Rev. A. Clerk.

Although at first opposed to Robert the Bruce, and swearing fealty to Edward of England, they latterly became stout champions of Scottish independence; one of them, in fact, marrying a sister of the Bruce.

Down to the period anterior to the struggles that led to the Reformation of the Church (I use the work Reformation here because Protestant historians have popularised the description, though a better phrase would be "Spoliation of the Church Lands"), down to that period the Lords of Argyll, though possessed of great territorial influence, had not figured very prominently in national affairs; but whether excited to Protestantism primarily by hope of Church spoil or by honest conviction, the Campbells undoubtedly played a leading part on the Anti-Popery side.

Mr. Howard Evans, actuated possibly by the highest motives, has been at some pains to dilate on the services some of the Argyll chieftains rendered to the cause of Protestantism, but he has not shown the other side to the picture. The "great" marquis of Argyll, whom Mr. Evans calls a "martyr," was a land thief and robber on a big scale; indeed, it is not at all improbable that the Highland clans who joined Montrose in his rebellion, were actuated, not by any love of the Stuarts, but by desperate fear and violent hatred of the rapacious "Grim" Archibald of Argyll. Dr. Cameron Lees, in his "History of Inverness-shire," says:–

> "When the Inverness-shire clans joined him (Montrose) they were attracted to his standard more probably from hatred to Argyll than from affection to King Charles. Gillespie Gruamach, or Grim Archibald, as they called that nobleman, was their dread foe. Ever since the downfall of the Lords of the Isles, his family had gone on acquiring territory in the West, *and was now threatening to add lands in Inverness-shire to its possessions*. Argyll had obtained the superiority of Loch Eil and of Glengary; that of Badenoch he had received from the Presbyterians. He *was credited with a scheme for the acquisition of all Lochaber. There was apparently no limit to his acquisitiveness . . . Had he been on the side of the King, they would probably have been on that of the Covenant*."

So that after all, his services to the Covenant were seemingly of somewhat negative value. Nor was he a particularly attractive specimen of the large-scale thief. Dr. Lees tells us that at the Battle of Inverlochy he kept carefully out of harm's way, and, watching the battle from a distance, incontinently bolted when his force was beaten, leaving his clansmen to their fate.

> "This same 'Grim' Archibald," says Bishop Burnet, "was a pretender to high degrees of piety, but he was a deep dissembler and great oppressor in all his private dealings, and he was noted for a defect in his courage on all occasions where danger met him. This had one of its usual effects on him, for he was cruel in cold blood; he was much set on raising his family to be a sort of king in the Highlands." †

And, again, the good Bishop declares that he "showed a very bloody temper"; many prisoners he had given quarter to, being afterwards murdered in cold blood. He was declared by Swift to have been "the greatest villain of his age," and he was not at all so keen on Protestantism, but he was prepared to sell it. He offered his own daughter in marriage to King Charles as "the properest match for him, not without some threats, if he did not accept the offer." Lord Lorn, his son and heir, to make sure that the family would succeed whichever side was finally victorious, took the opposite side, and when the father was executed at the instigation of Lord Middleton, who expected to grab the Argyll estates, Lord Lorn, the Anti-Protestant, had sufficient influence at Court to frustrate him.

Let me now retail the circumstances of the horrible and dastardly massacre of the Lamonts at the Gallows Hill of Dunoon in the year 1646 – a massacre that shocked and infuriated even a bloodthirsty Scotland, and was one of the chief counts in the trial which led to the beheading of the then Duke of Argyll. The Lamonts, or Maclamonts, had held Cowal from the dawn of Scots history, and their bards sang their descent from Somerled the ancient King of

---

† "History of His Own Time." Vol. I., p. 47.

Kintyre. The family had consistently supported the Stuarts; but in the 17th century when disaster after disaster to the Stuarts had culminated in the surrender of King Charles in 1646, the Campbells saw their opportunity. Three hundred years before, the Maclamont had foolishly allowed Argyll a site for a burying ground; that was sufficient footing for a Campbell. He had squeezed and elbowed himself into the proprietorship of half Cowal, and had seized the Castles of Dunoon and Carrick. The followers of the Stuart dynasty were exasperated at the encroachments of the Campbells,* and, under Montrose, proceeded after the Battle of Inverlochy, to crush the Argylls back from the stolen lands. Then came the surrender of King Charles and Argyll's opportunity. The Campbells surrounded Castles Toward and Ascog, and forced the Lamonts to surrender. The terms of the capitulation included a stipulation that every Lamont who surrendered should have his life spared; but the Campbells desired to exterminate, not merely to crush; they desired the lands of Cowal without contending claimants to perpetually trouble them; and so, despite their pledges, they set about murdering the prisoners. The indictment presented later against the Earl of Argyll for these atrocities sets the circumstances clearly before us. The prisoners were bound hands behind back like thieves, and so kept "for the space of several days in great torment and misery."

> "In pursuance of their farther villainy, after plundering and robbing all that was within and about the said house (Toward) they most barbarously, cruelly, and inhumanly murdered several – young and old, yea, sucking children, some of them not one month old."

Remember that it is these fiends whom our Protestant children are told to reverence as the honest upright Protestant nobleman who fought for the Covenant.

Thereafter the remainder of the Lamonts were taken to Dunoon. Thirty-six were hanged on the Gallows Hill; many others were simply "dirked"; the Provost of Rothesay got his throat cut;

---

* "The History of Cowal "—A. Brown, p. 57.

others were buried alive and given "no time to recommend themselves to God"; and since that time the Campbell family have reigned undisturbed and honoured in Cowal.

The Macnaughton lands were seized in somewhat novel fashion. About 1700 the Macnaughton Chief contracted to marry the youngest daughter of Campbell of Ardkinglass. After the marriage, that gentleman conjured his daughter out of the way, and substituted his oldest daughter in her stead in the "dark bridal room." Next morning Macnaughton discovered the trick and he and the genuine bride for very shame and fear fled to Ireland, whereupon Campbell seized the Macnaughton territory. The lands of Otter on Lochfyneside were wheedled out of the hands of the McEwans†.

> "When they got a footing at Inverary, they merely asked for as much as a cowhide would cover; but when they got this grant, they cut the hide into whangs, which extended over a wide territory." §

And that was truly typical of the Campbells. Greed, insatiate and unashamed, has been their hallmark.

The third Earl flourished as a politician in the gay "every man has his price" days of Walpole. He suppressed the malt tax discontents and was suitably rewarded. Under the Jurisdiction Act of 1747 he got his hands deeply into the public purse. For giving up the office of Justiciar of Argyllshire and the Islands, he did not scruple to take £15,000; as Sheriff of Argyll he annexed £5000, for the "regality of Campbell," £1000; in all, £21,000. He doubtless was of the opinion that there were easier methods of filling his purse than by working. On his death he left his real and personal estate in England to an illegitimate son. Succeeding Earls have "gone in" mostly for politics or military careers; but they have not shown to outstanding advantage in either profession. A recent Duke of Argyll achieved a certain reputation for sham philosophy, and the present one has married a Princess.

---

† "The History of Cowal," p. 52.

§ Ibid, p. 65.

In comparatively recent times their record as landowners has been a monstrous one. Their territory is too far from the cities to have enabled them to do much in the way of "holding up" for famine prices when waterworks, etc., were wanted. But what they have lost in this branch of spoliation they have adequately balanced by robbery of the poor Islanders. Let anyone who doubts this turn to the evidence given before the Crofters' Commission.¶ There he will find the rents in Iona raised in one swoop by 50 per cent in the year 1847 – a year of penury – and have been more than doubled since; there he will find the common lands stolen from the crofters in the year 1860. There he will find allegations that the crofters are forced to give the Duke's factor so many days' labour without reward. There he will find the Duke giving few fixed leases and collaring at sweet will houses which were built by the tenantry. There he will find the Duke's chamberlain making a most miserable and shamefaced appearance before the questions of the Commissioners. There he will find from Tiree despairing complaints, and details of horrible and dastardly evictions of blind men and *enciente* women. There he will find simple fishermen crying "We have neither law nor liberty." There he will find, in short, adequate reason to believe that the time has come to end this hereditary lord and land business, this, the greatest tragedy of our time.

¶ See particularly Vol. 4.

THE CAMPBELLS
OF BREADALBANE.

"The Scotch Highlanders will ere long disappear from the face of the earth; the mountains are daily depopulating; the great estates have ruined the land of the Gaul; as they did ancient Italy. The Highlander will ere long exist only in the romances of Walter Scott. The tartan and the claymore excite surprise in the streets of Edinburgh; they disappear – they emigrate – their national airs will ere long be lost, as the music of the Æolean harp when the winds are hushed."
> —*Michelet.*

"My own conscience is perfectly free. I never told anybody not to pay rent; I never told anybody to shoot landlords from behind a hedge; what I have stated is that it was a strange thing that the Irish, who were guilty of such things, should get lollypops, while the quiet Highlanders got stripes and nothing else."
> —*Professor John Stuart Blackie before the Crofters' Commission. Evidence, Vol. iv., p. 3286.*

"Some remove the landmarks; they violently take away flocks, and feed thereof. They drive away the ass of the fatherless, they take the widow's ox for a pledge. They turn the needy out of the way; the poor of the earth hide themselves together ... They cause the naked to lodge without clothing, that they have no covering in the cold; they are wet with the showers of the mountains, and embrace the rock for want of a shelter. They pluck the fatherless from the breast, and take a pledge of the poor. They cause

him to go naked without clothing, and take away the
sheaf from the hungry."　　—*Job, chap. 24.*

THE present Marquis of Breadalbane, I am given to understand, is
one of the broadest-minded and most humanitarian spirited
landowners in Scotland. Of course, this does not amount to much,
but it is as well to give credit where credit is due, and the present
Marquis is entitled to, at least, sympathetic recognition of the fact
that he differs widely from the ferocious, brutal, and unscrupulous
tyrants who previously held the title.

Possibly it is his family history, with its long records of pillage,
theft, and crime that drives the present Breadalbane to make
apologetic amends. At any rate his family fortunes are the result of
the most scandalous rapacity and tyranny; his ancestors are among
the most successful land thieves in Scots history, and the famous or
infamous evictions of less than a century ago forced even hardened
Tories like Sir Walter Scott to protest.

The Breadalbanes own about a quarter of all the land in
Perthshire, and in Argyllshire they own more than the Duke of Argyll
himself. The following table from the Landowners' Return of 1874
shows the lands held by the Breadalbane family: –

	Acres.	*Gross Annual Rental*
Argyleshire—		
Earl of Breadalbane	179,225	£21,165
Trustees of First Marquis of Breadalbane	24,967	1,150
Perthshire—		
Earl of Breadalbane	193,504	28,765
Trustees of first Marquis of Breadalbane	40,662	7,212
Garden Campbell of Troup	10,516	1,620
Banffshire—		
Garden Campbell of Troup	9,547	5,794
	458,421	£65,706

I do not know whether or not these figures include deer forest acreage;
if they do not, considerable additions must be made to the totals.

In the "Black Book of Taymouth" a valuable collection of Breadalbane documents and drawings published (for private circulation only) by the late Earl of Breadalbane, there appears a picture of a pious old mulatto coloured man, with long white wavy beard and hair. He is dressed in sea-green armour, leans on a huge sea-green sword, and stands over the words "Colin Campbell de Glenurquhart, Primus." This gentleman, a younger son of Sir Duncan Campbell of Lochow, was the founder of the Breadalbane family. He had been "granted" the estate of Glenorchy by his father; he "received" from the King the Barony of Lawers, and he acquired by his second marriage a portion of the lands of Lorne. This first laird still further added to his patrimony by open theft of the lands of Auchmoir, Ardtallonik, the "Port and Isle of Loch Tay," Innerneill, etc.

Let us look for a moment at the pillaging exploits of the second laird. I quote from the "Black Book of Taymouth," page 15*, but I have translated it word for word into readable English.

> "CONQUESIT. – The said Sir Duncane lived laird thirty-three years, during the which time he obtained tacks of the King's lands in Breadalbane, and of the Chartirhows lands lying within the same, the tacks of the 'tuelf' markland of Granduich."

> "Item, he conquesit † the heritable title of the barony of Finlarg — together with the bailzerie of Difcheoir, Toyer and Glenlyon, tane of the King, he annexit to the 'hows'."

That is plain enough. "He annexit to the hows," in other words, he stole the Crown property, and added it to his house or family possessions. Again: –

> "Item, he conquesit the threscoir markland of the baronie of Glenlyon, which he gave to his second son

---

* Account written 1598 by William Bowy, Official Scribe of the Family.
† Stole.

Archibald, together with the twenty-four markland
of the third of Lorne, which he took from the 'hows.'"

"Item, he conquesit the eight markland of Scheane
in Glenquoich, which he gave to his brother John
Campbell of Laweris to be held of the 'hows'."

Not to make the story overlong, suffice it to say that he also appears
among the Kilbryde land of Lochfyne, the lands of Dolour,
Aucharnside, etc. This "conquesiting" gentleman, we are interested
to learn, was killed on Flodden Field, and was buried beside the
Earl of Argyle, because they had fought (and stolen) "valiantlie
togidder."

Of the third laird of Glenorchy all we are told is that he
"kepit" all the conquests that had been left to him.

The fourth laird also kept "all things left to him by his worthy
predecessouris."

The fifth pirate, besides retaining the family plunder, added
by conquest the lands of Ardbeich, "which he left to the hows with
great riches and store."

Accumulator number six, Colin by name, "conquesit the
feu of the King's lands and Charterhous lands in Breadalbane." §
He also grabbed the lands of Auchlyne, Ardchyllie, Dowinche,
"togidder with the superioritie of McNab, his haill landis." Thus
passeth the McNabs as landowners. Then after he had swallowed
up the McNabs and their lands, he proceeded to steal the lands of
Stronmeloguhan and "ane auld ludging in Perthe" which

"as yit remains with the hows." He also stole the
lands of Edinambill, of Edinkip, and of Kingarth.

Of the seventh laird, Sir Duncane, we read that he "conquesit" the
land of Dounfallanders in Strathtay, the lands of Drumnoquheill

---

§ The tacks or fues had been held by his forefather, Sir Duncan.

and Drumquhaffill in Atholl, much land in the Menteith district, Portellen and district; also the barony of Glenfalloch, and the "easter quarter" of "Monzee," lying in Strathearn. Then more land in Strathearn and "ane grass roum" in Glenleidnaik; land in Glenloquha, Brayglenis in Lorne, lands from Lord Drummond, and Lord Perth, lands in Balquhidder and Glenquoich; and so on – pages of robbery, undisguised and unashamed. Nothing came amiss to him, glebes, islands, and glens, he swallowed them all, and his "hows" waxed splendid in the land. It is true that he paid cash for part of his additions, but he carried his piracy it seems to such a length that latterly the law laid hands on him and insisted on his paying to the State in fine the sum of forty thousand marks. But he rose to favour again and spent much time in chasing the Clan McGregor. In 1617 he was appointed Hereditary Keeper of the forests of Mamelorn, Bendasserly, Finglenbeg, and Finglenmoer. In 1627 he was given a "certaine quantitie" of land in Nova Scotia, though what he had to do with Nova Scotia is by no means clear; indeed, it is hardly likely that he knew where Nova Scotia was.

The next Laird, Sir Colin, seems to have been a patron of the arts, and to have spent much money in securing "reliable" title-deeds for some of the lands acquired or "conquesit" by his ancestors.

The methods by which the title of Earl of Breadalbane was obtained are somewhat interesting. It was in the days of the dissolute King Charles II and the Breadalbanes had become wealthy. They had, in fact, money to lend. The then Earl of Caithness was at that time in financial straits, and borrowed from the Breadalbanes, who drove a hard bargain with him. The whole estate and earldom of Caithness was to be handed over to the Breadalbanes in six years. The King was induced to confirm this "agreement" and when the six years had elapsed, the Earl of Caithness showed no disposition to hand over everything, title included, to the Scots Jews, the Breadalbane promptly raised an army to invade Caithness. This proceeding saw the origin of the well-known song "The Campbells are Coming." Latterly the King saw that public opinion was on the Caithness side, and induced the Breadalbanes to withdraw their claim to the title of Earldom of Caithness. In return for this magnaminity, the reigning Breadalbane was created Earl of Breadalbane of Holland, Viscount of Tay and Paintland, Lord Glenorchy, Benederaloch, Ormdie and Weick.

In Lee's "History of Inverness-shire," we are told that after one of the Stuart Rebellions, the Government, desirous of ingratiating itself with the Highland Clans, gave Breadalbane £20,000 to disburse among them. Needless to say, Breadalbane stuck to every penny – the Highland Clans saw none of it.

In the year 1853 Mr. Robertson, a Perthshire landlord, wrote a book entitled "Barriers to National Prosperity," and dedicated it to the well-known reformer, Patrick Edward Dove of Edinburgh. In it he made several animadversions on the scandalous evictions that had taken place on Breadalbane property. To this the Marquis of Breadalbane replied; and then Mr. Robertson followed with his detailed proofs and drove home his points with such stinging irony that the Marquis decided to invite no further publicity on the subject.

The substance of Mr. Robertson's charges was that at that time there were about 800 square miles of Scottish territory handed over to sport – to the killing of pheasants, grouse, or deer; that such territory could support 100,000 sheep and 10,000 black cattle, and that the Breadalbane policy since the beginning of the century had been to evict the small tenant, chase him away to the cities or across the seas, in order to make room for my Lord the Marquis and his autumn shootings. The country was being denuded of its brain and muscle; pauperism in the large towns was increasing; and misery and fear, due to insecurity of tenure, was bred in the lives of they who still laboured on the land.

"I can point," says Mr. Robertson, "to a place where thirty recruits that manned the 92nd in Egypt came from. . . Now only two families reside there altogether."

On a huge grazing farm that once supplied 100 horsemen, now only were left the grazier and one or two shepherds.

Greed is no respecter of persons, and some of the Glenquiech tenants whose families had been in possession for 400 years had been swept away. In Mornish 22 families were replaced by one. The Cloichran, once with eight or nine families, was now without a tenant at all. Acharn swept bare; the little farm "toons" practically cleared out; from lands that in 1793 the late Marquis had raised 1600 men for the French War, now, at the outside, only 150 could be got for military purposes; the forty families on the Braes of Taymouth and Tullochyoule cleared out at the point of landlord tyranny; on the Island of Ling only one family left, though at the beginning of the year in which Mr. Robertson was writing, there had been twenty-five families resident; the population of Glenorchy had been reduced from 1806 in the year 1831 to 831 in the 1841; *from the year 1834 to the year 1854 some 500 families were cleared off the soil!* The huge forest of Blackmount and the forest facing Kenmore, this latter the finest soil in Perthshire, kept waste for the sport of fashionable idlers; the tenants bound by terms of their lease to leave the fields near the deer forests under grass, so that the game might feed in winter – at the tenants' expense; tenants' gardens and crops destroyed by marauding and hungry deer, but no tenant to set dog or lift firearm to scare them away, lest he be ejected from his holding!

Freedom under Breadalbane landlordism, forsooth! Hear Mr. Robertson:–

> "I refer to the case of a tenant at Acharn, who was tempted to shoot a fallow deer, which had perhaps fattened on his crops or cabbage. The servant, instead of going to church on Sabbath, went to inform your Lordship's keeper of the occurrence; and if I am correctly informed, that worthy man went shortly after and made a search in the house. He was like to be foiled in the pursuit, when he took off the kail-pot and carrying it to the door, found therein a piece of

venison! What a horrible disclosure! The venison
was forthwith carried to Bolfracks, and such a hulla-
baloo was there! And what was the sentence? —*ban-
ishment!*"

Mr. Robertson is particularly severe on the Marquis as an employer
of labour.

"I am aware that your Lordship does give considerable employment to workpeople; but what kind of
wages do the regular workers get? *They travel some
three, four, and five miles to and from work daily, and the
scanty pittance they obtain is* $^1/_2$ *per diem in winter and* $^1/_4$
in summer. By the time an able-bodied man pays house
rent out of that sum, and keeps a family, he cannot
hoard much money in the banks!"

So that it will be seen that Mr. Robertson takes a somewhat different
view of the possibilities of thrift from our favoured placemen, Lord
Cromer and the Hon. John Burns!

These evictions, of course, are scandalous from any point of
view; but when one remembers that under the old Celtic Clan
system the lands were not the absolute property of the Chief, but
were the property of the Clan, vested in the Chief, who had no
legal or other right to dispossess the clansmen: no legal right to
evict, no legal right to appropriate rents, no legal right to do
anything but govern the interests of his clan—when one remembers
these things, he is justified in adding the charge of wholesale robbery
to the indictment of the Breadalbanes and their kind. Mr. Hill
Burton calls the procedure by which the Lords obtained power to
dispossess the clansmen, "iniquitous legal jugglery," and he has
by no means used extravagant language in his description.

THE CAMPBELLS OF CAWDOR.

It is recorded that:–

> "When Egypt went down, two per cent of her
> population owned ninety-seven per cent of her
> wealth—wealth is the wrong term here; it should be
> 'property'—the people were starving. When Persia
> went down, one per cent of her population owned all
> the land. When Babylon went down, two per cent. of
> her population owned all the wealth—should be
> 'property' again—when Rome went down, 1800 men
> owned all the known world."
> —*"Foundations of Political Economy,"*
> *p. 14. W. Bell Robertson.*

> "If the impotent creatures perish for lack of necessar-
> ies, you are the murderers, for you have their inherit-
> ance . . . If the sturdy fall to stealing, robbing, and
> revenge, then you are the causes thereof, for you dig
> in, enclose, and withhold from them the earth out of
> which they should dig and plough their living."
> —*Robert Crawley (Archdeacon of Hereford.)*

THE present Earl of Cawdor sits high in the councils of the Tory
Party, was a member of the last Tory Government, and although he
is, comparatively speaking, at least, only one of the smaller fry of
Scots land rent drawers, he as chairman of a railway company and
as a representative of the "sly, sleekit Campbells" exercises a
considerable influence among Tory working men.

The family fortunes of Lord Cawdor are founded on the
abduction of a child heiress, and by judicious selection of wealthy

wives they had had acquired at the time of the last Landowners' Return*, lands in Scotland and England as follows:–

	Acres	Gross Annual Rental
Nairnshire	146,176	£7,882
Inverness-shire	3,943	1,738
Cardiganshire	21	
Pembrokeshire	17,943	35,024
Carmarthenshire	33,782	
	101,857	£44,644

The Earl of Cawdor has also acquired considerable landed property in the United States of America.

The origin of the ancient family of Calder is lost in the mists of antiquity. Originally the Calder Chief fulfilled the duties of toshach, *i.e.*, administered the Crown lands and acted as headman for the district, and it is not till the time of Malcolm Canmore that we hear of a Calder being called Thane. In 1405, we know that Andrew of Calder or Cawdor, was hereditary sheriff and constable of the King's Castle there. We guess of course that there must have been considerable "pickings" in the former post, but the latter office seems purely a nominal one. Still, when it was abolished in the 18th century, the Campbell who then held the sinecure managed to extract £2000 in compensation from the pockets of the British people. William, the Sixth Thane, was a hanger-on at Court, and extracted some "privileges" (*i.e.*, powers to rob the people) from the King.

At Cawdor Castle they once showed the room where Duncan was murdered by Macbeth, and "a series of wretched daubs on the whitewashed walls of the apartment"† doubtless added to the apparent holiness of the relic. But, like the "true nails of the Cross,"

---

* The story is well told in Mackenzie's "Tales and Legends of the Highlands," p. 132.
† "Moray and Nairn." C. Rampini, LL.D., p.251.

which the manufacturers of the Middle Ages turned out, it is now only jeered at. Duncan was, in reality, not murdered, and the Castle in any case was not built until hundreds of years after his death. In 1492 a Cawdor married a daughter of Rose of Kilravock. This pair had a daughter, Muriel, who fell heir to the family estates. It seems that Muriel's parents died when she was an infant. Here was a glorious bone for the dogs to snarl over. The Earl of Argyll's cupidity was excited, and being a powerful man at Court, he succeeded in getting the wardship of the child. He got old Rose of Kilravock (the grandfather) to consent because that aged worthy had got himself involved in a charge of robbery, and only through Argyll's good offices could he escape punishment. Then Argyll recommended his third son, John, to go up and take both the acres and the infant as his own. There was evidently opposition to this, offered by the old grandmother, who, to make sure that no changeling business would be attempted, branded the child on the hip with her coffer. Argyll's son, however, arrived on the scene with a small army of Campbells at his back, and after some parleying, grabbed the child and bolted back for home. The old lady immediately aroused her friends, and the Campbells were hotly pursued, but they managed to escape. It was during the flight that John Campbell is reported to have given weary utterance to the proverb "Tis a far cry to Loch Awe. Far is help from Clan Dhuine!" The infant, whose hair is said to have been pronouncedly red in colour, was safely landed at Inverary, and so eager was John Campbell to "mak' siccar" the lands, that he married the child when she was only 12 years of age.

During the child's infancy her abductor was asked what he would do if she died before he could marry her, and consequently before he could lay his hands on the Calder estates. The answer was a truly Campbell one—"The child can never die so long as there is a red-haired lassie to be found on either side of Loch Awe." Impersonation was infinitely easier than abduction.

After he married the child, he assumed the title of Sir John Campbell of Cawdor, and proceeded forth to add to his possessions by means which other land thieves resented, and for which he was haled before the law courts. One of his sons is described in an old MSS. quoted in the Statistical Account of Scotland§ as being a valiant, witty, and active man who bribed a priest to bribe the Bishop of the Isles to hand over the "right to this barony and regality of Kilmoranag or Country of Muckairn, which the said priest did carefully manage." The "said priest" also cleverly obtained "the Pope's confirmation to the right, which was done by his legate, Sylvester Danus, the last legate from the Pope in this kingdom."

One of his sons became in 1573 Bishop of the Isles. "He dilapidated," says Keith in his 'History of the Scottish Bishops,' "most part of the benefice in favour of his relations," and the reverend gentleman who writes the article on Ardchattan in the Statistical Account of Scotland, says: –

> "What had been appropriated for ages to the support of religion, was thus dishonestly converted into private property, a common occurrence at the Reformation in Scotland, and a few individuals were enriched by that which should, on no principle of justice or of expediency, have belonged to them."

In 1726 a Campbell of Cawdor married a Welsh heiress, Mary, daughter of Pryse of Gogirthen, and there being more money in Welsh rents than in Highland Scots ones, shifted his family seat to the new plunder ground, leaving a factor behind in Nairnshire. Campbell, of course a Tory, got himself into Parliament in the days before Welshmen had votes. His descendant still draws rent because the people who pay the rent have not the sense to use their votes wisely, and because they still somehow believe that land rent is taken by divine right and not by mere descent from unscrupulous thieves and rogues.

---

§ P. 513, Vol. VII.

THE BRUCES

(LORD BALFOUR OF BURLEIGH AND LORD ELGIN).

"Strong Churchmen, sirs, we ought to be,
Since we sit on the lands,
And fatten on gear
That once belonged to the Abbey."

AS a land firm the Bruces are to-day of small account, though at one time they sat on the Scots throne and handed away Crown lands with lavish generosity. In 1874 they held: –

	Acres	Gross Annual Rental
Clackmannanshire—		
Lord Burleigh	943	2,003
Lord Burleigh (Mines)	–	904
Fifeshire—		
Lord Burleigh	349	834
Earl of Elgin	2,663	8,370
Earl of Elgin (Mines)	–	3,710
Perthshire—		
Lord Burleigh	1,393	766
Earl of Elgin	232	1,870
	5,580	£18,457

There were also cadet branches owning between them other 13,000 acres, with a rental of £20,000.

"About the year 1050 divers noblemen of Normandy, coming over with Queen Emma, settled themselves in England; after her death (being hated of the English) were forced to retire to

Scotland."* Among these foreign adventurers, hated presumably with good reason by the English, was one De Bruis or De Bruce, who also, it appears, assisted William the Conqueror in the plunder of England, for he swallowed many manors and lordships. One of De Bruce's sons married the heiress of Annandale, and received from King David a charter of her lands, to be held on a "tenure by the sword." To assist him in this tenure came knights and yeomen from Yorkshire, among whom appear to have been the progenitors of the Carlyles, the Jardines, and the Johnstons. We are told that he died in 1141 "an old and opulent man." In 1271 a Bruce married the Countess of Carrick (the marriage was in the King's gift) and in 1306 as everybody knows, Robert Bruce became King of Scots.

And here is the long and short of the origin of the Clackmannan estates of Lord Balfour of Burleigh.

> "King David Bruce in . . . 1369 gave the Barony and Castle of Clackmannan, which of old belonged to the Crown, to his kinsman."†

That is to say, the Clackmannan estate (Crown or public property) was handed over to an ancestor of Lord Balfour's, merely because that ancestor was a favourite at Court. The Bruces who at an early period married themselves into the Balfour title have not distinguished themselves either by extraordinary ability or shameless rapacity, although I see that a Burleigh got his hands on £2000 as compensation for the loss of his Hereditary Sheriffship of Kinross. The fifth Lord, who murdered a schoolmaster bridegroom because he (Balfour) had taken a fancy to the bride, wound up his ignoble career by being attainted for participation in the Rebellion of 1715, and the attainder was only withdrawn in 1870.

The Elgin branch is also founded on a Royal grant. In 1603

---

* Family Tree of Bruces of Clackmannan, quoted in Old Statistical Account. Vol. 14, p. 637.
† Ibid 641

The Bruces

King James gave the lands of Kinloss Abbey to Lord Edward Bruce, a direct ancestor of the present Earl of Elgin. The family also thankfully "received" the ecclesiastical lands of Rosyth, the barony of Pittencrieff, Poldynnes, etc. A Bruce was created Earl of Elgin by the dissolute King, Charles I, but since that time most of the family prosperity has been the result of heiress-marrying. The third Earl married the heiress of the Seymours, and got much land in Wiltshire, and another married a wealthy Dutch heiress.

Both the present Lords Elgin and Burleigh have "gone in" for politics, one as a Liberal, the other as a Tory, and neither seem to have starved in the process.

Lord Burleigh draws £100 a month, having as an ex-Cabinet Minister signed a plea that he was too poor to do without some State help. This pension does not, however, seem to have destroyed his energies or his capacity for thrift, for he "directs" some 7 public Companies (total capital over £88,000,000), engaged in banking, rails, steamships, and telegraphs. In his spare time he amuses himself with the pleasantries of the Anti-Socialist League, endeavouring to revive antedeluvian political theories. He was wildly excited over the introduction of an old-age pension of five shillings per week to working class octogenarians, believing that State pensions destroy self-reliance and individuality. He left us to infer that he spoke from personal experience.

THE KERRS.

"Our present land laws, by which a monstrous accumulation of landed property in the hands of a few is
artificially encouraged, are, historically considered,
merely a badge of conquest from the Conqueror down-
ward, maintained and cherished by every device that
the love of power, the pride of pedigree, family vanity,
and the ingenuity of lawyers could invent."
—*John Stuart Blackie.*

IT appears that not only the wicked but their descendants are allowed
to flourish like the green bay tree. Here, in the Kers, we have the
descendants of savage pirates, men who literally washed their hands
in blood, men who stole without ceasing, and murdered without
compunction, rewarded generation after generation with an annual
payment of £145,554! The last Landowners' Return showed:–

	Acres.	Gross Annual Rental.
Berwickshire—		
Innes of Ayton	5,780	10,949
Duke of Roxburghe	6,096	876
Haddingtonshire—		
Duke of Roxburghe	3,863	4,662
Edinburghshire—		
Marquess of Lothian	4,547	11,918
Marquess of Lothian (Mines)	–	6,296
Kirkcudbright —		
Ker of Argrennan	959	1,265
Roxburghshire—		
Ker of Sunlaws	2,662	3,154
Duke of Roxburghe	50,459	43,820
Marquess of Lothian	19,70	23,684
	94,106	£145,554

The founder of the Ker estates seems to have been a huntsman or forest-rover, who was taken under the patronage of the Douglases, and was, for some reason or other, given a charter of the lands of Altonburn and Nisbet. In 1451, James II gave the Kers the lands of Auldroxburgh "for payment of one silver penny at Whitsunday if demanded," and in 1488 James IV handed over "Roxburgh with its patronage of the *Maisondieu*"* for payment of "a red rose at the feast of St. John the Baptist." It is well to have these accounts exact; they may be useful when the State demands restitution and the Duke makes an outcry for "compensation." The two supporters on the Roxburgh crest are "savages, each holding a baton," and I can imagine nothing more appropriate, for with the Scotts and other robber clans, they were eternally at feud, and they carried their moonlighting and murdering right up to the streets of Edinburgh.

At the Reformation of Church Plunder period, the Kers absorbed the whole of the great property of Kelso Abbey, miles and miles of rich lands, baronies, lordships, mills, patronages, everything they could lay their hands upon, and the sole excuse given for this shameless rapacity is that "Sir Robert Kerr of Cessford was a great favourite at Court."† These estates are to-day enjoyed by Sir Robert Kerr's descendant, although we are told in Crawford's "Peerage," that the Kers were forced to hand back about 20 churches and their tithes to the Crown. The first Earl was Privy Seal to Charles I, was notorious for his cruelty, and was long remembered for his disgraceful betrayal of Montrose. They specialised in open rapine, these Kers. So late as 1620 Sir George Douglas reports:–

> "They came to the commontie of the burgh called Kaidmuir, where some of the inhabitants were occupied in their lawful affairs upon their own heritage, and thair threatnit theme with death gif they depairtit not the ground, and did what in them lay to have broken His Majesty's peace."

---

* House of God.
† Jeffrey's "History of Roxburghshire." Vol. III., p.83.

In 1747 they were busy abstracting coin from the public exchequer, and as compensation for loss of hereditable jurisdiction of Kelso, they took £1300, for Sprouston, £300; and for Ancrum, £500: in all, £2100. In 1812 the title devolved on Sir James Innes, the main stock having failed. The Inneses make a boast that they are happy in three things:–

> That no inheritance ever went to a woman;
> That none of them ever married an ill wife;
> That no friend ever suffered for their debt.

The present Duke has married an American heiress, and gives as his family motto—"Pro Christo et Patria dulce periculum". ("Sweet the danger for Christ and country.") Imagine it!

The other branch of the Kers, which persists to-day in the Marquess of Lothian, has for progenitors, the finest collection of knaves and cut-throats to be found in Scots landed family history. Here we have the infamous "Dand" Ker, who, in 1515, stormed Kelso Abbey, and turned the Superior out of doors, here we have "Dand's" son, the dissolute Viscount Rochester, who married the divorced Countess of Essex, and who, in 1616, with his degraded wife, treacherously murdered his friend, Sir Thomas Overbury; here we have "Habby" Ker, the grim humorist, whose castle precepts were "Feir God: fle from Sin: mak for the Lyfe everlasting to the End," but whose trade of murder and hanging made him regarded with almost superstitious fear by his contemporaries; and here we have the Sir Andrew Ker (first Lord Jedburgh), who was charged at Edinburgh, in 1601, with the slaughter and demembration of large numbers of Turnbulls, Middlemasses, and Davidsons. A fine portrait gallery this of the Marquis of Lothian! The Jedburgh Abbey estates (stolen from the Church) were excambed from the Earls of Home. Newbattle Abbey was "acquired" direct at the Reformation, and Jeffrey tells us that the seventh Marquis "annexed to his estates on the Border, Bongedworth, Tempendean, Crailing Tofts, Ormiston, and Harden Peel." The Lothian crest is "The Sun in its Splendour," and the motto "Sero sed serio" (Late but in earnest).

THE STEWARTS OF GALLOWAY.

> "The dissolution of the monasteries, etc., and the appropriation of the lands without any legal or formal rights by those . . . who pretended to support the Reformation, but more for selfish purposes than religious . . . We refer specially to Galloway."
> —*McKerlie, "Galloway, Ancient and Modern," p.240.*

THE history books of our school-days supplied us with many fictions, but on no part of our national records have they woven more ridiculous and romantic nonsense than on the Norman conquest. William the Conqueror is represented as landing at Hastings with the chivalry and nobility of France at his back, and since that chivalry and nobility ravaged England, stuck to the lands of the dispossessed natives and swarmed into the House of Lords, I suppose it is necessary that we should early be taught to worship their descendants, lest we should ask "why and wherefore have these men rule and doninion over us?"

Alas, that I should shatter a delusion; but it is necessary that the truth be told. The Norman Conquerors were not mostly "of blue blood "; they were as McKerlie, the historian justly says, "the scum of France "; they were led by one William surnamed the Conqueror, who was an illegitimate son of a Duke of Normandy by the daughter of a tanner in Falaise; and they simply "Murdered, stabbed and grabbed" their way to affluence. Among the menials in this devouring horde was one named Flaad. This Flaad had a son Alan, who was stationed at Oswestry to push his fortune in Scotland, where King David I (or as he was called the 'Monk-Feeder') was waiting open-armed for all varieties of foreign mercenaries who should help him to dispossess the Church of Iona and substitute in their possessions the Church of Rome. Walter entered the personal service of the King as *dapifer* (dish-bearer or waiter) and gradually rose to the position of *steward* or keeper of the revenue. When there, says McKerlie,* "The fortune of the family was made. Lands were secured as the superior of, and others as actual ownership, in various districts." Frequently they acted the part of traitors, and we must remember that it was a grandson of the third High Steward who for £100 of land betrayed Wallace. Finally, a Steward (or Stewart) married Princess Marjory, daughter of King Robert I, and so began the Stewart race of Kings. The fourth High Steward, Alexander, had already secured the lands of Garlies in Galloway, which had, it appears, been stolen from the Ionan Church for the purpose of enriching Court favourites; and to these lands his second son succeeded. This second son is the ancestor of the present Earl of Galloway. The family motto is "Virescit vulnere virtus" (virtue flourishes from a wound). The family wounds must have healed quickly. The Stewarts applied for £6000 as "Compensation" on the abolition of hereditary jurisdictions; but even a landlord-ridden Treasury would pay no more than £321 6/. The Galloway estates have been much depleted, but in 1874 they stood at:–

	Acres.	Gross Annual Rental.
Kirkcudbright—		
Earl of Galloway	55,981	£7,333
Wigtonshire—		
Earl of Galloway	23,203	24,864
	79,184	£32,197

---

* See History of Galloway, Vol. IV., p.369. P. H. McKerlie, F.S.A., F.R.S.S., Etc.

THE STUARTS OF BUTE.

"For the needy shall not always be forgotten."
—David the Psalmist.

"Land is not and cannot be property in the sense that
movable things are property; the land of any country is really the property of the nation which occupies
it." *—Froude.*

THE Marquesses of Bute are the unhappy victims of a huge family
joke. The joke lies in this: that while the family motto is "Avito
viret honore"—"he lives or thrives on an honourable ancestry"—
the family itself has sprung from *one of King Robert II's nineteen
illegitimate children.** There is a tradition, says Burke's "Peerage,"
that the mother's name was Leitch, but nothing more is known
about her. King Robert—licentious rascal though he was—looked
well after his fly-by-night progeny, and to provide for this son of
his, Sir John or "Black" Stuart, he erected in 1385 the Islands of
Bute, Arran, and Cumbrae, into the County of Bute; appointed
"Black" Stuart Hereditary Sheriff of the new County, and made
over to him huge grants of land. It is very difficult, indeed, to trace
exactly how the long line of Stuart sheriffs managed to eat up the
smaller land-holders in the District, and Reid, the historian, only
touches the subject gingerly when he says:–

"The land-holders in the County gradually dimin-
ished in numbers, in consequence of the absorption
of many of their properties by the larger heritors."

* See "History of the County of Bute"—J. E. Reid, p. 194.

Of course, Reid's "History" is dedicated to the Marquis, so that one would hardly expect to find in his pages any illuminating sidelights on the particular forms of land robbery practised in Bute. There appears to have been only one member of the family who stepped into the public arena, and it would have been better for the nation if he had stepped earlier out of it. John, 3rd Earl, flourished after the '45 Rebellion. He attached himself to the Court party, and got mixed up in all manner of intrigues. Through Court influence he was appointed one of the Secretaries of State, and in 1762 was actually given the office of First Lord of the Treasury. Then he commenced a long, scandalous and deliberately-planned system of bribery and corruption. Sometimes a House of Commons division cost him £25,000, but he had command of the public purse, and was doing splendidly until he began the erection of a huge mansion in London, and set himself extravagantly and ostentatiously to spend huge sums of money on art treasures wherewith to decorate and beautify his new home. Then the people got suspicious that Bute was "tarry-fingered" in his Treasury transactions, and he was hounded from office by popular clamour. He was a suave, cynical, polished rascal, and did not hesitate to buy addresses of approval from any Town Councils and Magistrates who were open to bribery. He was unsuccessful with a bait of £14,000 to the Corporation of London; but other towns yielded to the temptations of his money bags; he left behind him wherever he went a trail of rascality and corruption; and he did his utmost to lower and degrade the whole public life of the country. Mr. Massey, the historian, declares that had he lived in sterner times he would have lost his head, so shameful were some of his transactions. When, in 1747, the Act to abolish hereditable jurisdictions was passed, he asked £8000 compensation for loss of his Sheriffship and regality of Bute; but even a landlord controlled Exchequer squirmed at such rapacity, and latterly fobbed him off with £2186 9/3.

In searching for particulars of the Bute Family history, I came across rather an interesting fact, and one that deserves publicity.

From November 26th, 1660, till the Act of Union the Burgh of Rothesay paid its Member of Parliament two merks Scots per day as allowance or salary. Of course, this was a sound principle, so long as the M.P. could only be a large landowner, but, nowadays, when the hod-carrier can, if the people so wish, become a legislator, it would appear to be necessary to throw cold water on the agitation for the payment of Members, and to suggest that it would mean moral and financial shipwreck.

The Bute Family has not greatly distinguished itself in any way beyond showing a happy instinct in the marriage market. It has ever had a keen scent for heiresses and successful marriages; and it has acquired thereby huge mineral and port revenues at Cardiff, an estate in Wigtownshire, and an estate in Ireland. At the time of the last Landowners' Return (1874) the Butes were shown owning lands in Scotland as follow:–

	Acres.	Gross AnnualRental.
Ayrshire —		
Marquess of Bute	43,734	£22,756
Marquess of Bute	–	2,506
Buteshire—		
Marquess of Bute	29,285	19,606
Kirkcudbright—		
Earl of Galloway	55,981	£7,333
Wigtonshire—		
Marquess of Bute	20,157	2,936
	93,176	£47,804

In addition to this he has over 25,000 acres in England, rental almost £200,000; while Lord Wharncliffe and Lord Stuart de Decies, two other noble fledglings from the Bute nest, own between them nearly 60,000 acres, rent roll over £51,000. This is neither the reward of industry, thrift, nor ability. It is the reward of Royal license, heiress marrying, and easy access to the public pocket.

THE KENNEDYS

ROASTING THE ABBOT.

THE Kennedy or Cassilis Family, the present representative of which is the Marquess of Ailsa, acquired its landed property by means best described in the one word—brigandage. The founder of the clan appears to have been one of the foreign swashbuckling adventurers who accompanied King Malcolm when he came to Scotland, and he received grants of land in Ayrshire from that monarch; probably in return for military services rendered. The general attitude of the Cassilis family to other people's property, and the methods by which that property was "contrived" into the Cassilis hands is evident in the history of the theft of the lands of Crossraguel Abbey.

When the storm of the Reformation swept over Scotland, the monks of Crossraguel, besides the Abbey itself and a well-appointed town-house in Maybole, owned or ruled (or both owned and ruled) eight parishes and twenty-seven manors.

John Knox, the graceless iconoclast, wrecked the Abbey; but Gilbert Kennedy, Earl of Cassilis, cared little about the building; it was the parishes and the manors that excited his cupidity, and so he seized the Abbot (one Alan Steuart), and conveying him to the Castle of Dunure, demanded that all the parishes and manors should be signed over to the house of Cassilis. For a long time the Abbot stoutly refused to sign away the Abbey property, but Cassilis meant business, and he proceeded to roast the Abbot over a slow fire. Latterly the poor abbot succumbed and signed the necessary document. In due time when the story of the Abbot-roasting had excited great indignation in Scotland, the Privy Council took the matter up, and demanded security for the future good behaviour of the Earl; but that rascal was really too powerful for the Privy Council, and so the "proceedings" gradually fizzled out, leaving Crossraguel, its manors and parishes in the hands of the Cassilis Family. This theft of the Crossraguel lands occurred in the year 1570, but some eleven years previous to that the Abbot, "to secure a powerful protector in the coming storm," had named the Earl as Heritable Bailie of the district. The Kennedies held this office till 1747, when they had the impudence to claim £12,100 compensation upon the State deciding to abolish the sinecure. Of course they did not get £12,100; but democratic opinion was not so strong then as now, and the Parliamentary Commissioners awarded £1800—which, of course, was £1800 too much. The Kennedys, though still exercising considerable Conservative influence in Ayrshire, have nowadays only a comparatively small land holding, returning their annual spoil in the year 1874 as follows:–

	Acres.	Gross Annual Rental.
Ayrshire—		
Marquess of Ailsa	76,015	£35,825
Marquess of Ailsa (Minerals)	–	14
Kennedy of Dunure	4,142	6,895
Forfarshire—		
Kennedy Erskine of Dun	1,727	3,571
	81,884	£46,305

The family is at present "sitting tight," and evidently resolved to make the State pay dearly for any land it may require and demand for lighthouses, etc. It will be remembered that in the year 1883, when the Commissioners for the Northern Lighthouses took over 5 acres of land on Ailsa Craig for the purpose of building a lighthouse, they had to pay no less than £1550, though the land in question had previously been returned at no value whatever. The

Cassilis motto is "A vis la Fin," a free translation of which is "Hang on warily to the end." I commiserate with them on the fact that the end is near.

Here is the story in Old Scots, as it is given in the "History of the Kennedys," in Bannatyne's "Memoriales," and in the Statistical Account of Scotland, Vol. V. (Sec. Maybole), p. 359:–

"Efter the Erle" saw "that he culd not come to his purpose be fair means, he comandit his coockes (cooks) to prepare the banquet. And so fust, they fleed the scheip, that is, they took of the Abbote's cleathes, even to his skin; and next, they band him to the chimlay, his legges to the one end and his armse to the uther; and so they began to bait the frye, sometymes to his buttockis, sometymes to his leggis, sometymes to his shulders and armes. And that, the rost shall not burne, but that it might rost in soppe (soup), they spared not flambing with oyle (Lord, luik thou to sic crueltie). And that the crying of the miserable man suld not be hard, they closed his mouth, that the voice myght be stopped. In that torment they held the poore man; while that oft tymes he cryed 'for Gode's sake to despatch him.' . . . They perceiving the rost to be aneugh, comandit tit to be tane fra the fyre and the Erle himself began the grace in this maner: 'Benedicte Jesus, Maria! You are the most obstinate man that ever I saw' . . . And yet he returned to the same practeis within two days and ceased not till that he abteaned his formest purpose; that is, that he had gotten all his pieces subscryvit, alsweil as one half-rosted hand culd do it."

THE HAYS

(LORDS TWEEDDALE, KINNOUL, AND ERROL).

> "Wherefore feed and clothe and save
> From the cradle to the grave,
> Those ungrateful drones who would
> Drain your sweat—nay, drink your blood."
> —*Shelley.*

THE Hay Family history begins with a Norman butler in the service of Malcolm IV, and is simply a long record of successful marriages and wheedling of land charters from Kings. This Norman butler, William de Haya, contrived to marry a daughter of Ralph de Soulis, Lord of Liddesdale, who is referred to in Douglas's volume in the County History Series as one of the most remorseless tyrants in Border history. Lands in Locherworth were received in 1238 by a fortunate marriage with an heiress of the Lindesays. In 1296 great estates in Peebles were got through a matrimonial alliance with an heiress of the Frasers. In King Robert's time they seem to have been busy absorbing Royal "grants." In 1420 another fortunate marriage was arranged with an heiress of the estates of Giffard and Yester. In 1594 the ecclesiastical lands of Bothanes were secured. Indeed, the Tweeddale branch seems to have been continuously absorbent, without resorting, so far as I can discover, to actual physical force. The motto of the butler's progeny is "Spare Nought!" but they seem to have dealt in flattery, sycophancy, and marriage manipulation rather than in murder and open pillage. In 1385 they got a share of the 40,000 francs bribe sent across by the King of France with John de Vienne to corrupt the Scots nobility (which needed no corruption), and when hereditary jurisdictions were abolished, they impudently claimed £8000 for loss of the Bailliery of Dunfermline. They got, I regret to say, £2672 7/. The Marquesses of Tweeddale have never shone in public life, unless we except the eighth holder of the title, whom the peerage writers describe as one "possessed of great sagacity and attention to business; opposed the Act for regulating the Appeal of Churchmen, 1633," and of the next holder they can say nothing beyond the fact that he "always studied to keep proceedings in a legal channel, and was for moderate councils."

The family crest, I see, is "A Goat's Head erased." The goat's head I can understand, but why the "erased"?

The following table shows their land holding in 1874. The cadet branches are omitted:–

	Acres.	Gross Annual Rental.
Aberdeenshire—		
Earl of Errol	4,249	£4,268
Berwickshire—		
Marquis of Tweeddale	18,116	9,572
Haddingtonshire—		
Marquis of Tweeddale	20,486	11,485
Perthshire—		
Earl of Kinnoul	12,577	14,814
Roxburghshire—		
Marquis of Tweeddale	4,425	4,774
	59,853	44,913

The Kinnoul branch has been quite as greedy as the Tweeddale one. The first representative of the Kinnouls was a "sponger" at the Court of Charles I. He contrived to marry the heiress of Lord Denny, and on her death made a clandestine match with a daughter of the Earl of Northumberland. This lady, says Douglas's "Peerage," "was the reputed mistress of Pym." The Earl of Kinnoul was everything that was detestable, and in a Court noted for voluptuous living, was singled out for dishonourable mention.

The King gave him the Island of Barbadoes, and some £400,000 of public money,* yet he ran through it all and died in poverty. He invented Ante Suppers,

> "The matter of which was to have the board covered, at the first entrance of the guests with dishes as high as a tall man could well reach, filled with the choicest and dearest viands sea or land could afford. And all this once seen, and having feasted the eyes of the invited, was in a manner thrown away, and fresh set on to the same height, having only this advantage, that it was hot."

We read "of a whole pie" composed of ambergreece, magisterial of pearl, must, etc., being carelessly thrown to a menial," and the menial eating it all! The early Kinnouls were Royalists; the later seem to have all been presidents of societies for the propagation of Christian knowledge. In 1747 they asked £3000 for the loss of their regality of Balhousie, but had to be satisfied with £800.

The Errol branch were also great place-hunters. The Aberdeenshire estates and the hereditary Constableship of Scotland were conferred on Sir Gilbert Hay by King Robert Bruce. The tenth Earl, in King Charles II's time, lived so extravagantly that the Errol estates in Perthshire had to be sold. In 1747 the then Earl asked for £5000 for loss of his regality of Slains, but only succeeded in mulcting the State to the extent of £1200. The family motto: *serva jugem*, does not imply that the Errols consume their liquor from plebian pots of earthenware. It means "Preserve the Ox-Yoke."

---

* "Douglas Peerage," Vol. II., p. 45.

THE GRAHAMS.

"I came of the Graemes—a people of ancient and hot blood."   —*Scott.*

"They come to church as seldom as the 29th of February comes into the calendar . . . They resemble Job, not in piety and patience but in sudden plenty and poverty; sometimes having flocks and herds at night, and none in the morning." —*Fuller.*

THESE quotations do not refer to the present Duke of Montrose, who seems (as will hereafter appear) to have pensioned himself comfortably on the rates of Glasgow, but to the Clan Graham in General.

The De Graemes originally were swashbucklers at Court; they were brave warriors, and in return for their services with the sword, various monarchs handed them over the "right" to draw rents from huge tracts of land. Their headquarters were in the neighbourhood of Dalkeith, but one sept or branch seems to have migrated to the Borders, where it levied blackmail and raised ferocious "bobberies" equal to those raised by the best and most capable freebooters of the period.

In Alexander II's time, Sir David de Graham appears as receiving grants of the lands of Kilpont and Ilkeston in Linlithgowshire, and from him are descended the families of Menteith and Montrose. A Graham married a daughter of King David, and was created Earl of Strathearn (later creation: Menteith), and from these two were descended all the long race of unfortunate and debt-embarrassed Earls, who chose, seemingly with unerring accuracy, the losing side, and who lost their Earldom with the tragic death of the "Beggar Earl" at the side of an old dyke near Bonhill. They seem to have been constitutionally incapable of "making money";* history attributes to them no scandalous massacres or robberies of the poor.

Later Stuart Kings feared them, for they boasted "the reddest blood in the land," and their existence as the direct descendants of King David, and the lineal heirs to the Stuart throne, rendered them a perpetual menace to the existing regime. They were, therefore, suspected and feared, crushed, snuffed, and beggared out by the more powerful Stuarts, who had collared the throne. The direct descendant of the Earls of Menteith, in the male line of succession, is Mr. R. B. Cunninghame Graham; and those who have the personal friendship and acquaintance of the intrepid Socialist leader, have often hugged themselves as they visioned the occurrences that would of a surety arrive, were the Stuarts to return to the Scottish throne in the person of the man who wrote "Success," and who went to gaol for the unemployed.

The Montrose branch, although it also has famous—and deservedly famous—men on its roll, men like the Marquis of Montrose, a nobleman in the truest sense of the word, though his fame has been tarnished by bigoted Protestant historians—the Montrose branch, especially in later years, has developed the catchpenny and plundering instinct we have had so frequent occasion to remark upon in these histories.

The Stuarts might fall, the great Marquis who fought so stoutly for them, might be ignominiously beheaded, the title may be attainted, but somehow or other a successor would recover the estates and wheedle back the title. Every Scotsman knows the story of "Rob

---

* The pathetic side of their history is graphically depicted in Mr. Cuninghame Graham's "Notes on the District of Menteith" and, more concisely in Burke's "Vicissitudes of Noble Families."

Roy" Macgregor, the bonnet laird whom the Duke of Montrose foreclosed upon and hunted out to the wilds as a freebooter—chased out, as Nimmo says in his "History of Stirlingshire" in a manner "inconsistent with the rights of humanity." Everybody knows how Rob Roy turned on the Ducal robber like a wolf at bay, how he lay regularly in wait for the Duke's factor to despoil him of his rents, how he prevented Ducal plundering of the poor. And everybody knows the cause of Macgregor's plaintive wail:–

"We're landless, landless, landless, Gregalach."

I cannot discover precisely how the Montrose family acquired all its lands. The Buchanan estate seems to have been genuinely purchased from creditors of the Buchanans in 1682; we know how the Macgregors were brutally rooted out; and Nimmo declares that huge tracts were received at various times in grants from successive Kings. At anyrate by the year 1874 they had collected a land area as follows:–

	Acres.	Gross Annual Rental.
Argyllshire—		
Graham of Skipness	15,000	£1,876
Dumbartonshire—		
Duke of Montrose	2,588	1,807
Duke of Montrose (Quarries)	–	30
Perthshire—		
Graeme of Inchbrakie	5,088	3,211
Graeme of Garvock	644	844
Graeme of Meiklewood	688	1,166
Graeme of Overglenny	300	100
Graeme of Cultoquhey	2,519	3,117
Graeme of Netherglenny	479	172
Graham of Murrayshall	1,913	2,678
Graham of Coldoch	400	696
Graham of Devonshaw	503	490
Duke of Montrose	32,2994	5,556
Duke of Montrose (Quarries)	–	133
Stirlingshire—		
Graham of Gargunnock	288	514
Graham of Strathblane	1,205	423

Graham of Dalquharn	547	558
Graham of Airth	1,145	3,141
Graham of Airth (Minerals)	–	100
Graham of Ballagan	914	612
Duke of Montrose	68,878	15,706
	135,393	£42,927

There are other small landowners of the name of Graham; but I cannot clearly trace their connection with the Ducal house. They include Graham of Ferenze and Graham of Craigallion; and in recent years the Marquis of Graham, the Duke of Montrose's heir, has added no fewer than 102,210 acres (rental, £18,702) in Buteshire, by his marriage with Lady Mary Hamilton.

The "Leabhar dearg" or Red Book of Menteith, is sparse in its clues to plundering of the public purse, but I see from a Graham family history, entitled "Or and Sable,"* that when heritable jurisdictions were abolished in 1747, the Duke of Montrose claimed £15,000 compensation for loss of his Sheriffship of Orkney. What he was doing up in Orkney is by no means clear, but it must have been a source of great grief to him that the State refused to pay a penny more than £5578 18/4. I like that 18/4. There is a strict matter of fact equity, and letter of the law justice about it that somehow seems to disguise the barefaced and impertinent robbery of the £5578.

In later years the attacks on the public purse have been continuous and direct. Listen to this: it is an extract from a speech delivered by ex-Bailie Burt, of Glasgow:–

> "The people of Glasgow wished to extend their water supply at Loch Katrine, and had to make use of a piece of waste land there. He did not suppose any sane man would offer for this land more than a shilling per acre per annum. It supported some Highland cattle and a number of sheep, but he never saw anything else on it. But seeing that the land was re-

---

* P. 504.

quired for public purposes it might have been thought that they would be expected to pay 40 years' purchase and add 10 per cent compensation for compulsory purchase. That would work out at 42/ per acre, but the Duke of Montrose actually refused £72 per acre . . .

"On the occasion of the annual trip to Loch Katrine, following upon the Corporation dinner, a discussion took place with the factor of the Duke of Montrose as to the rate Glasgow charged to outside burghs for supplying them with water, and, of course, outside burghs were charged a higher rate than the inhabitants of Glasgow. The factor observed that the Corporation were making an excellent profit by selling the water to the surrounding districts, and thought he should have a bigger share of the plunder. Within 12 months afterwards it was intimated that the Duke proposed to give feus for building purposes on the shores of Loch Katrine. Of course, to have villas there, and possibly sewage going into the loch, was something which the Commissioners could not contemplate. The result was that an appeal was made and the Duke of Montrose had to be paid £25,000 additional plunder for giving up the right to feu. It was quite possible that the Duke never really intended to have villas there, and was only anxious to get a little more of the plunder."

What did it matter to him whether the citizens of Glasgow were sewage-poisoned or not? But, like the jungle tiger, his desires grew with what he fed upon, and early this year (1909) the Corporation of Glasgow requiring to raise the level of Loch Arklet by 22 feet right round the swamp, marsh, barren land and rocks which border the water, he sprung a claim for £26,000. Of course the Corporation laughed at the claim, but when the dispute went to compulsory arbitration, the Duke walked off smiling with £19,090 4/5, the citizens of Glasgow paying all expenses of arbitration. Still, that was not all. He "stipulated" that the Corporation must keep good the road (nine miles) from Inversnaid to Stronachlacher "for all time coming," make and keep up new roads and paths, maintain farm fences, look after drainage and sewage of his farms in the vicinity, reconstruct his boathouse and lay down proper appliances for his boating excursions (this last includes "beacons" lest he run aground). When it transpired that material would be required to raise the loch level, and that an overhead ropeway was necessary to tranship the material from Loch Lomond to Loch Arklet, the Duke appeared with an extra claim for £1525 in respect of possible injury to shooting rights. This figure, he declared, he had arrived at on the understanding that the ropeway was to carry no more than 20,000 tons of material, and was to be taken down in three years. If more was carried or the ropeway left up for a longer period, additional and proportional payment was to be made. And as a sort of afterthought he decided to ask that the temporary supply of water laid into the hotel at Inversnaid be left undisturbed for all time at no cost to him.

From all which it will be seen that the tribe of the daughter of the Horse Leech who cries continually "Give! Give!" is not yet extinct, and one wonders what would happen if the Duke could contrive some legal claim to the atmosphere. The Duke is a Tariff Reformer, but he is not in favour of disturbing the existing land tariffs.

THE FRASERS.

"William the Norman, improperly called the Conqueror,
invaded England at the head of forces mixed and collected from many countries, most of them needy adventurers, allured by promises of plunder and settle-
ments in this Kingdom, which when subdued, was to be
turned into spoil and parted amongst the spoilers. . .
He seized a great number of estates with as little ceremony as mercy. When by this, and every furious oppression, he had made the miserable nation stark mad,
his next step was to punish them for being so. He therefore, besides infinite vengeance, corporal and capital,
at once seized into his own hands, all baronies, and all
fiefs of the Crown. Thus he reduced all the nobility and
landholders in England to nakedness and want of bread
. . . Their estates were granted to favourites and champions of the Usurper, desperate adventurers and the
needy hunters of fortune. These upstarts and spoilers
were incredibly exalted. Some of them rioted in the
revenue of whole counties; many of them counted their
manors by hundreds. Others were made Lords of Cities, others proprietors of great towns; the rest commanded strong forts and castles, now purposely built to
secure the everlasting bondage of the wretched English
. . . He (William) extended his savage scheme to the
English clergy, despising their privileges, trampling on
their charters, and subjecting them to what burdens he
pleases, and put Normans in their room. Some he banished, others he imprisoned, and supplied all the va-
cancies with strangers, creatures of his own or of the
Pope. Such was the return to the English clergy for
their early submission to him, and their treachery to
the country."   —J. Peele, 1747.

126

THE Fraser family has to-day a comparatively small holding of land in Scotland, and as it has not, in recent generations at anyrate, crossed the path of democracy, we need spend but little time on its history.

Among the adventurers and pirates whose names appear on the roll of Battle Abbey, as having crossed the channel with William the Conqueror to subdue and plunder Britain, is one surnamed Frizel; and it is certain that the Frasers or Frizels ravaged their way up to Teviotdale shortly after the Conquest in 1066. By judicious marrying of heiresses they attained considerable wealth and influence; and when, about the end of the 13th century, Sir Andrew Fraser married a daughter of the Earl of Caithness, the Fraser family was safely on its feet. Through his wife, who was heiress of the Grahams of Lovat, he acquired vast lands in Inverness-shire. Quite at an early stage in their career as land magnates the Frasers showed a special disposition to acquire Church lands. In 1377 Hugh Fraser appears to have been in trouble for his remissness in handing over to the Bishop of Moray, rents which should have gone to the Church, and at the Reformation period the then Lord Lovat added to his estates the "Priory of Beauly and the lands belonging to it." This included the town and lands of Beauly, the lands of Ardnagrask, Rhindouin, Inchrorie, Craigscorry, Platchaig, Groam, Farley, with its forest and woods, Teachnuick, with its pendicles of Ruilick and Greyfield, Elschany, part of Culmill, Glenconvinth, and Fanblair, the whole lands at Annat, Teafrish, Mills, and the whole fishing rights from Cairncot to the sea. The Abbot, Sir Walter Reid, appears to have been party to this swindle, for he sold Lovat the office of hereditary Bailie of the district "for two silver pennies at the feast of Pentecost, if asked," and I should be surprised to hear that when hereditary jurisdictions were abolished, Lovat did not demand and receive huge monetary compensation from the State for loss of his "right." The Lovat who flourished about the time of the Stuart rebellion of 1715 was a notorious rascal. Bishop Burnet tells us that he was "accused of a rape on a sister of Lord Athol's for which he was convicted and outlawed." He then went to the Court of St. Germain, "and pretended he had authority from the Highlanders to undertake to bring together a body of 12,000 men," to upset Queen Anne's Government, and restore the Stuarts.

The French Court dallied with the rascal, and gave him some information. He then "got himself secretly introduced to the Duke of Queensbury, to whom he discovered all that had been already transacted. . . he also named many of the lords who opposed him most in Parliament, and said they were already deeply engaged." He also "faked" a letter addressed to Atholl from France, and handed it to Queensbury. He was then engaged as a spy by the British Government, and succeeded in getting many innocent people into trouble. One rejoices to know that he was finally beheaded.

The estates were forfeited to the Crown, and the title attainted. But the most thorough-paced rascal of all the Frasers, was Simon, the thirteenth Lord, who, though he began his life under a cloud, and with his father's estates forfeited to the Crown, yet succeeded in recovering both the estates and the position which his father, the Government spy, had lost. This Simon was a sycophant of a detestable type. He crawled and cringed before, and flattered unashamedly the people in high places. He begged the forfeited estates of the Chisholm and Glengarry, who had been "out" in the "fifteen" rebellion. He pled earnestly that they should receive no pardon for their misdeeds; and he seems in 1716 to have succeeded in wheedling out of Duncan Forbes of Culloden, all the estates of the hapless Mackenzie of Fraserdale. He stuck at nothing to further the success of his schemes, and the story of how he managed to marry himself into the powerful house of Argyll, is happily uncommon even in the annals of our titled rascality.

It was necessary for the furtherance of some project of his that he should have the favour and protection of the Campbells of

Argyll. To achieve this he decided to marry Primrose, sister of the fourth Duke of Argyll, but the lady abhorred him, and refused his offers with contempt. Still the honourable Fraser bided his time; he could afford to wait, until one luckless day, when visiting a relative, Miss Campbell received an urgent note purporting to come from her mother, beseeching her daughter's immediate presence at a certain house in Edinburgh, where the mother lay at the point of death. Miss Campbell, we are told, started at once for this place, and was met on arrival with every show of respect,

> "But instead of being shown into her mother's chamber as she expected, she was brought face to face with the special object of her aversion, Lord Lovat, under conditions which impelled her to listen to his vows of endearment. She, however, continued obdurate, until her heartless suitor told her that she was in a house of ill-fame; and it is said that the disclosure which he threatened in this connection and a confinement of several days within the walls of such a place, ultimately overcame her resolution. She was only 23 years of age, while he was 66."*

Off such fine strains come our blue-blooded nobility; and I cannot for the life of me understand why the Saltoun branch of the Frasers, well known, and accordingly, disrespected in Aberdeenshire, should possess sufficient calm impertinence to flaunt as a family motto the words "In God is all," and to expose on their family crest the figures of two angels!

At the time of the last Landowners' Return the Fraser family land-holding totalled as follows:–

	Acres.	Gross Annual Rental.
Aberdeenshire—		
Lord Saltoun	10,782	£11,929
Frasers of Williamston, Findrack, Castle Fraser and Sheddocksley	7,677	7,218

* Mackenzie's "History of the Frasers" (p. 443).

Inverness-shire—		
Lord Lovat	162,048	28,219
Frasers of Abertarff, Ardachy, Farraline, Kilmuir, etc.	83,159	13,507
Perthshire—		
Fraser of Blackcraig	2,722	1,537
Ross-shire—		
Fraser of Glastullich	660	611
Fraser of Arabella	625	995
	267,673	£64,010

THE RAMSAYS

(LORDS PANMURE AND DALHOUSIE).

"Those merciless devourers of the patrimony of the Kirk."
—*John Knox.*

AMONG the noble families living to-day on gratuities annually paid under the title of land rent, are several whose comparative unimportance absolves us from the devotion of much space to their misdeeds. One of these families is the Ramsays, whose progenitor—an obscure German pirate—came over in 1066 with the sweepings of the Continent in the train of William the Conqueror. He, or more probably his son, took military service under David I and as usual with these mercenaries, doubtless lived by robbing the natives. At anyrate, the Ramsays became notorious border raiders, and were always in demand when throats were to be cut. They acquired large estates through marriage with an heiress of the Maules, a family of Norman mercenaries who had also been hired by King David, and who had secured royal grants of land in Midlothian and in the Carse of Gowrie. The first Earl Panmure also obtained many royal grants from James VI; but the whole family fortunes fell with the downfall of the Stuarts, and but little was saved from the wreckage. It is to a Dalhousie we owe the annexation of the Punjaub, Berar, Pegu, Napore and Oude, and all the countless blood and treasure these conquests have since cost us. The family landholding in 1874 was:–

Edinburghshire—	*Acres.*	*Gross Annual Rental.*
Earl of Dalhousie	1,419	£3,002
Earl of Dalhousie (Mines)	–	450
Forfarshire—		
Earl of Dalhousie	136,602	55,601
	138,021	£59,053

THE HAMILTONS

AND THEIR MINING ROYALTIES.

"What myght be done with money and rewarde he coulde not tell, for the capitaine of the Castell of Edinburgh is one of the Hamyltons, which he said be all false and inconstante of nature."

Letter from Sadleyr to Lord Suffolk and others.
"The Hamilton Papers," Vol. II., p. 90.
Ed. By Joseph Bain.

"Regarding Royalties, I can almost be certain that a few landlords in Lanarkshire reap more benefit from the mines than upwards of 30,000 miners."

R. Steele (Miners' Agent).
Evidence before Royal Commission,
1890. P. 112, Vol. II.

"The Duke of Hamilton receives in royalties £143,000 a year, his dead rents running from £500 to £50,000, and additional royalties from 9d. to 1/6 per ton of coal raised."

London Daily News, May, 1909.

IN the year 1874 the Hamilton Family returned itself as "owning" lands and drawing rents as per the following table:–

	Acres.	*Gross AnnualRental.*
Earl of Selkirk (Kirkcudbright)	20,823	£19,769
Earl of Haddington (Haddington)	8,302	13,678
Earl of Haddington (Berwick)	14,279	15,099
Earl of Haddington (Lanark)	501	588
Earl of Haddington (Roxburgh)	4,708	5,079
Lady Mary Hamilton (Arran)	102,210	18,702

Lady Mary Hamilton (Haddington)	14,345	24,537
Duke of Hamilton (Lanark)	45,731	38,441
Duke of Hamilton (Lanark) Minerals	–	56,920
Duke of Hamilton (Linlithgow)	3,694	7,445
Duke of Hamilton (Linlithgow) Minerals	–	8,076
Duke of Hamilton (Stirling)	810	911
Duke of Hamilton (Stirling) Minerals	–	2,011
Duke of Abercorn (Renfrew)	496	1,680
Duke of Abercorn (Renfrew) Minerals	–	2,307
Duke of Abercorn (Paisley)	166	733
Lord Belhaven (Lanark)	2,078	4,674
Lord Belhaven (Lanark) Minerals	–	19,521

That is to say, the Hamilton Family plunder Scotland annually to the extent of £247,571, and they "own" 219,643 acres. The Arran estates have now fallen into the hands of the Montrose family, since Lady Mary married the Marquis of Graham.

But I have not shown you all the family revenues. In 1874 the late Duke had an estate in Suffolk of 4939 acres, gross annual rental of £8017. This is, I fancy, also the property of Lady Mary. And in the same year (1874), the Duke of Abercorn owned in

	Acres.	*Gross Annual Rental.*
Tyrone	47,615	£25,420
Donegal	15,942	10,382
Sussex	8	9

In addition to all that there are about other nine Hamiltons with estates in Great Britain, showing a total approximate acreage of 126,000 acres.

But it must be remembered that these figures are for the year 1874, and that the enormous development of the mineral wealth of Lanarkshire since that time will have vastly augmented the amount of the unearned income, which the people pour so lavishly into the Hamilton exchequer. Indeed, I am well within the mark in saying that the descendants of Walter Fitz-Gilbert, who broke his pledged word and sold his trust to his King's enemies, now exact from the people of Great Britain in land plunder alone half-a-million pounds sterling every year. Mr. Robert Smillie, the miners' agent, has publicly declared that the present Duke of Hamilton's mining royalty is about 8d. per ton.

"I have heard it put," (he says) "that in the bad year of 1879, when miners were starving, the late Duke's royalty rents were about £120,000—more than all the coal-getters got for hewing coal that year."

His Grace the Duke of Hamilton has more titles than any honest man has need of; he is Duke of three places, Marquis of as many; Earl of four, and Lord of eight; besides that he is the Premier Peer of Scotland, and the Heritable Keeper of Holyrood House, the Lord-Lieutenant and many other dignities too numerous to detail.

The "one side of the house" he comes of the noble Freskin blood—blood which seems to have scattered itself well over Scotland, for it founded, as we have seen, the Atholl and the Sutherland families. And now we find that a progenitor of the ancient House of Douglas was a brother or some relation of this same Freskin, who did not number among his many faults that of seeing his relations go unprovided for. The present Duke of Hamilton is a descendant of the Douglases; but as his family tree runs straight back to an even more ancient stock of rascality than the Douglases, we will leave the Douglas records alone in the meantime.

When the Norman pirates landed at Hastings in 1066 and butchered King Harold, and as many of his nobles as they could lay hands upon, one Robert of Mellent distinguished himself among the invading ruffians. For his valour King William assigned him:–

64 Manors and Lordships in Warwickshire.
16 Manors and Lordships in Leicestershire.
7 Manors and Lordships in Wiltshire.
3 Manors and Lordships in Northamptonshire.
1 Manor and Lordship in Gloucestershire.

The religion of the times, as will be expected, did not worry *him* much, and we find him excommunicated by the Pope Pascal for some seizure of the revenues of the See of Canterbury.

His son and successor, the second Earl of Leicester and Mellent, first appears as a plotter engaged in some conspiracy to place the Norman crown on the head of the King's nephew. The plot was unsuccessful, but King Henry graciously pardoned the plotter and restored to him his estates, and he, Leicester, returned thanks by the energetic support he gave the King in the latter's struggle with Thomas a Becket, who "with contumacy and disrespect," and holding up a cross led "a tumultuous crowd of the lower orders."

The third Earl also engaged himself in unsuccessful plottings to depose King Henry. Again a Leicester was pardoned, and his estates returned to him.

One of the sons of this worthy—named Walter Filius Gilberti, or Walter Fitz-Gilbert—seems to have murdered another pirate who rejoiced in the name of Despencer, and as the Despencers "were a powerful family," the offender skipped off to Scotland, where he appears, heaven knows how, to have almost immediately acquired great possessions in lands and baronies. Among these were the baronies of Cadzow or Cadyow and Machanshyre; the lands of Edelwood in Lanark; the lands and baronies of Kinniel, Larbert, and Auldcathie, in Linlithgow, and the lands of Kirkender and Kirkowen in Wigtown. One account states that the hunted one arrived when the Scots King was at the head of a hunting party, and how he proceeded to complain that his troubles were the result of his battling for the honour of His Royal Highness. And then the grateful King soared into verse:–

> "Enough, enough, Sir Gilbert, we give thee welcome here;
> Look round thee, and where'er thine eye traverses far and near,
> These acres broad shall be thine own."

Naismith, in his "History of Hamilton," offers, however, a seemingly more reliable and plausible story. Walter had been appointed keeper of Bothwell Castle for King Edward I, and had in 1296 sworn fealty to that monarch; he also held many "lands" from him. Immediately the news of the English defeat at Bannockburn arrived, Walter evidently reached the conclusion that he was in danger of being on the losing side. English nobles arrived breathless. Walter received them beneath the English flag, and when he had got a sufficient "bag," promptly forgot all about his oaths of fealty to the English King, and handed over Castle and prisoners to King Robert the Bruce. For this signal piece of duplicity and treachery he was granted the lands aforementioned—lands which had been forfeited by "the Cumyns and other adherents of England," who were either too honest to turn traitor to their erst-while Sovereign, or were too late in making up their minds on the matter.

And so far as any authentic record goes, this is the sole reason given for the planting of the dukes with the many titles on the backs of the Lanarkshire people; it is the sole reason for these enormous Royalties that the obliging miner picks from the bowels of the earth for behoof of Hamilton Palace.

The Hamilton history is the history of most of our "noble" families, with this peculiarity, that if there was any dirty, low, sneak-mean-thief treachery to be done, a Hamilton would do it. The relation of one instance will be sufficient. About 1452 the Hamiltons and the Douglases were in close alliance and practically dictated terms to the King. Douglas, however, was treacherously murdered (S. R. Crockett has a very stirring account of it in his novel, "Black Douglas"), and Hamilton for some time, with the other powerful adherents and friends of the Douglases, carried fire and sword through Royal Territory in reply. But the King (James II) gradually recovered the upper hand, and no sooner did the crafty Hamilton see this than he called his kinsmen and followers "quietly together," and "carried them over to the Royal Camp and was received by the King with open arms, but, for the sake of appearances, was sent to

Roslin Castle for a few days." Result—Granted part of the lands of the now forsaken Douglases at Drumsagard, Carmunnock, and Fynnart in Renfrewshire, and other spoil; created a Lord, gets his clutches on the lands of Draffan from the monks of Lesmahagow and Kelso, and on land at Bothwell, Crawfurdjohn, Linlithgow, Kirkcudbright, etc.

Buchanan states that the aged Lord Hamilton in 1474 married Princess Mary, eldest daughter of King James II, and that this lady had been forced to forsake her legal husband, Boyd, Earl of Arran, for the purpose! Thus did the House of Hamilton "wed into Royal blood," and it is not strange that with the lady came the "lands and baronies" of Arran. Pretensions were now made to the throne of Scotland, and the third Lord Hamilton acquired the suggestive habit of signing himself "James G." or simply "James." Latterly he was forced to resign his offices in return for the Duchy of Chatelherault in France; King Henry II evidently thinking that "James G." was in fair way of becoming a strong rival to the infant Queen Mary.

In 1639 a Hamilton—a Royalist of course—attempted to invade Scotland with English troops, and it was on this occasion, that his mother, Ann Cunningham, appeared on the sands at Leith and threatened to shoot her son if he dared to land and attack his countrymen.

It would take a volume, not an article, to show how the Hamiltons spread their branches over many fat baronies and lands. Ill-fated Stuarts might go, the Macgregors be but a name whispered in fear; but the House of Hamilton, through fair weather and foul, now on one side now on the other, scattered their numerous septs of Abercorns, Belhavens and Stentons, Haddingtons and the rest securely on the backs of the Scottish people. And although here and there a Hamilton shines out honestly and bravely against the general darkness and duplicity of his House, although one Duke chivalrously spends a fortune to aid a scheme of Robert Owen's, there still remains the fact that the ducal greatness was founded in treachery, and that in the words of Sadleyr "they be false and inconstante of nature."

At one period of the family history, when Kings were squeezable, and popular rights totally disregarded by the landowners, the Hamiltons—almost every generation of them—managed to extort a grant of an abbey or a military or ecclesiastical office from the Crown. Most of these "grants" have been turned into hard cash long ago; and now the Abbey and the Abbot of Aberbrothock, in Forfarshire, the rich Abbey of Paisley, etc., own no sway to Hamilton Palace. Yet, as a family, the Hamiltons still retain the privilege of "holding up" Great Britain annually to the tune of over half-a-million sterling. These privileges, I repeat, are quite apart from their questionable legality, entirely immoral, since they are the results of treachery and the rapacious extortion of successful sycophants at Court; and, in any case, surely we and our succeeding generations will refuse to homologate these plunder bargains on which neither we nor our forefathers were consulted, and which simply consisted in one man (the King) assigning to another man (a Hamilton), the right *for ever* to plunder the people! By that bargain we decline to be found, and we must agitate till the people of Scotland insist that these mining royalties go, not to private pockets, but to the public purse.

When on this question of Mining Royalties, may I refer any miner who wishes further to study the matter to the second volume of the evidence before the Royal Commission on Mines (1890-1891). He will there find the Duke of Hamilton's factor, Mr. James Barrowman, admitting that the statement that the Duke's Lanarkshire mineral rental was between £60,000 and £70,000, "was not far wrong," (p.327) and that this sum was less than one-fifth of the annual mineral rent of Lanarkshire!

He will also find stories of the stoppage of Flemington and Letterick coal pits for a time, because of excessive Royalties:

he will find industries abandoned because the land drones sucked away too much in way-leaves and royalties (e.g. Brandon Malleable Iron Company in 1887.*)

He will find the Duke taking 3/6 per ton of Royalty on gas coal. He will find Lord Hamilton in 1887 taking 1/ per ton of "Royalty" for doing nothing, while the miner, who risked his life and gave his strength to win the coal, got only $9^1/_2$d. He will find in 1879 the same noble Lord sucking away 1/3 in Royalty, while the miner for his arduous toil got only 1/3. He will find in 1885, Watson, of Earnock, the lessee of a Hamilton coalfield, paying the miner $9^1/_2$d. and the Duke 1/4 per ton. He will find that the aforementioned factor could not suggest, though repeatedly questioned on the point, anything that the Hamiltons had done or given that they should be allowed to continue this perpetual plunder. †

And he will find in the evidence of the late Mr. William Small,§ who knew more about mining Royalties than any of his contemporaries, that *as a strict matter of legal fact, the Act of 1592, which lays it down that the minerals of Scotland belong to the Crown, has never been repealed, and should hold good in law even to-day.*

Mr. G. D. Hardie estimates that the Duke "pins" every third hutch of coal for "Royalty," and he says that "when No. 4 Watsonville Pit was started, the smoke chimney stood six feet above the trees, and could be seen by the Duke from his windows. It was an eyesore, and had to be cut down." There is a *soupçon* of comedy, intermingled with much tragedy, in this spectacle of the aesthetic Duke living in luxury on the toil and weariness of the man underground, but objecting to the size of the smoke chimney.

---

*   P. 108.

†   P. 326   .

§   P. 114-117   Ibid.

THE HOMES
AND THE DOUGLASES.

"And they flashed the spear and they stole the gear,
And they cleared the kine from Tay to Tyne,
And that's how they a' thrive, man."

THE present Earl of Home is not only the heir of the Homes, but he is the possessor of the remains of the great Douglas estates which at one time practically covered the South of Scotland. The present Earl owns but a tithe of the lands once held by the Homes and the Douglases, yet as will be seen from the following table, he is still able to get bread and butter in land rent, and, although unemployed, has not yet applied to a Distress Committee:–

	Acres.	Gross Annual Rental.
Ayrshire—		
Countess of Home	2,271	£1,367
Berwickshire—		
Home of Milne Graden	9,992	17,110
Earl of Home	2,597	5,244
Countess of Home	7,804	7,602
Home of Bassendean	775	890
Forfarshire—		
Countess of Home	5,209	7,356
Lanarkshire—		
Countess of Home	61,949	24,795
Countess of Home (Mines)	–	4,716
Renfrewshire—		
Countess of Home	1,325	3,463
Roxburghshire—		
Douglas of Chesterhouse	1,356	1,771

Douglas of Springwood	5,568	6,730
Douglas of Cavers	9,840	7,937
Home of Softlaw	605	1,059
Countess of Home	25,380	7,995
	134,671	£98,035

There are also the Douglases of Craigs, Banks, Lockerbie, Strathendry, Orbiston, Lesmahagow, and Lord Sholto Douglas, owning between them other 19,210 acres; rental, £28,779.

Let us take the Home Family first. They sprang from Ada, an illegitimate daughter of William the Lion, and take their name from the barony or parish of Home in Roxburghshire. The lordship of Dunglas was acquired by marriage in Robert III's time. Though vassals of the Earl of March, they gradually became a factor to reckon with among the Border reivers and when the star of Douglas was in the ascendant, they basely deserted March and fought against him under the Douglases. Indeed, they rose to eminence on the falling fortunes of their Chief; and they acquired a detestable reputation for instability and treachery. The Lord of Home got the Sheriffdom of Berwick from Moray for supporting his seizure of the Regency; yet in 1569 he basely deserted Moray for the Queen, and he stuck at nothing (from murder down) to fatten the revenues of his house.

Let me tell briefly the story of Coldingham Priory;* it will illustrate the special peculiarities of the Earls of Home. At the time of Robert III the Priory possessed extensive lands, and the Prior to protect himself against the depredations of the local titled rascality, sought the protection of the Earl of Douglas, who appointed Alexander, Laird of Home, as "Under Keeper" of the revenues, at a yearly salary of £20 Scots. The Homes had got a grip, and they held on with dogged pertinacity till the whole Priory was their own, though several generations had to pass ere the "transfer" was properly completed. In 1422, George, the third son of the aforesaid Alexander, was appointed Bailiff, and shortly afterwards, two rascals,

---

* See Chambers' "Caledonia," Vol. III., p. 329.

Patrick and John Home, who described themselves as Canons of the Church of Dunbar, intruded themselves on the unwilling Prior and his moneybags.

For twenty long years they "sponged" on the Prior, though he had even, in his desperation, got the sentence of Rome invoked against them. But just as the clutch of the Homes threatened to strangle the Priory, King James I annexed the whole property to the See of Stirling.

Then the wolves showed their teeth. They opposed the transfer by all means in their power, fair and foul (mostly foul), and succeeded in being indicted by Parliament in 1487 for treason. But they stirred up much opposition to the good-natured King, and until he was killed at Stirling in 1488, the Homes, smarting under the loss of Coldingham, were foremost among his most bitter enemies.

Then one Robert Blackadder appears to have got the Priory, but almost immediately he, "with six of his domestics," was murdered by Sir David Home "the outlawed murderer of De la Bastie (a Frenchman), with the help of the other Homes, who were fleshed in cruelty."

Then Sir William Douglas stole the demesnes, and in 1541 the Prior was discharged in order to make a vacancy for John Stewart, the infant illegitimate son of James V. "During," we read, "the infancy of the Prior, the King enjoyed the revenue."

John Stewart left two sons, Francis and John, "who did little honour to their family or service to their country."

Francis was finally created Earl of Bothwell, Abbot of Kelso, Constable of Haddington, Sheriff of Berwick, Bailie of Lauderdale, and High Admiral of Scotland; and the Earl of Home was "granted" Coldingham. In 1600 the Kirk made a vigorous protest against the theft; and Home, on being threatened with excommunication if he did not return the stolen lands, made an abject and degrading apology on his knees. But it was characteristic of him that he stuck to the Abbey lands. The Lord Home who flourished about the beginning of the 16th century was appointed Lord Chamberlain, and being desperately wicked, fulfilled the scriptures by blooming like the green bay tree. Chambers† describes him as venal; he "engrossed vast power and tried to amass great property," and Queen Margaret wrote to Henry VIII. "Home has assumed all the power and has seized the escheat (estate) of a bastard, which was estimated at £10,000 Scots."

His downfall, however, was near. An unsuccessful attempt to abduct the King; enforced exile to England, from whence he made periodic forays on the cattle of poor Scotsmen; pardoned; accused again of treason, and executed in 1516, his estates being retained by the Crown till 1522, when they were foolishly returned to the Homes by the Regent Albany.

To properly write the history of the Douglases would be to write the history of Scotland from the beginning of the 12th century till the Union of the Crowns; and for reason of space, we may only glance at it. First of all the reader is asked to forget all the romantic tales about the origin of the Douglases, which the S. R. Crocketts have so manfully striven to popularise. The first Douglas was not a "black grey man" who sprang miraculously from nowhere to assist a King in difficulties; he was a Flemish mercenary and adventurer, called Theobald, who was given lands on Douglas Water in 1147 by the Abbot of Kelso. The Abbot badly wanted a watch-dog in these troublous times, and Theobald was as serviceable as any. Theobald's descendants in course of time signed themselves "of Douglas," and when in 1270 the then Abbot parted with further land to them, they were firmly fixed as a "noble" family. The early Douglases married themselves carefully into neighbouring estates, and never parted with an acre once they had got their hands on it. Theobald himself, being somehow related to Freskyn, the land pirate

---

† "Caledonia," Vol. III., p. 288.

mentioned in previous papers, this grasping tendency is understandable; and in time the family became a bye-word even among professional and titled rascality.

> "As of Henry VIII it may be said of Douglas the first Earl, that he never spared man in his anger or woman in his lust."§

The "Good Sir James"—if all histories are to be believed—a valorous and honest sort of man, rose with the success of Robert the Bruce. Under Bruce, they over-ran the South country, and under David they over-ran the West, simply by accumulation of grants of forfeited estates. They held practically a Royal Court, created knights and rendered themselves objects of suspicion and jealousy to the Stuarts. Finally, after a long combat with the Crown that had enriched them, they were evicted and their estates forfeited in 1455. The old stock of "Black" Douglases however reappeared in the "Red" in the person of the Earl of Angus, who received the estates, and finally in 1859 the remainder of their lands were swallowed up by the Earl of Home when he married the daughter and heir of Lady Douglas Montagu. Whatever sneaking admiration a modern may have for these Douglas pirates whose lives were expressed in the family proverb, "It is better to hear the lark sing than the mouse cheep," he cannot regard the present day little field tyrants with anything but the most inveterate hostility.

On his Forfarshire estates the Earl of Home is still charging vassalage dues; he still exacts tribute for four weeks every year from the stalls in Kirriemuir market place, and it is only recently that he levied 2d. on every pound of butter, and 4d. on every dozen of eggs that went in to market. Down in the Upper Ward of Lanarkshire, his tyranny is even more scandalous and unbearable. Some of the miners who work at Glespin and who reside in Douglas, three miles away, were returning recently from their work in a hired waggonette when they met the Countess of Home airing herself in

§   "Caledonia," Vol. III., p. 120.

her carriage. The rude miners did not sing "Rule Brittania!" or cry "Hoch!" They did not wave cambric handkerchiefs, they simply stared; and so, next day came to the carriage-hirer from the Castle a request that in future he should hire no waggonette to the miners. It is intolerable that colliers should drive; it is intolerable that their dirty faces should come between the landscape and her nobility; and to remove the injustice, the miners of Douglas now tramp the moor, six miles of it per diem, singing, I hope, "Britons never shall be slaves!"

The Earls of Morton are also Douglases, being descended from a younger son of the second Earl. The Morton crest is, appropriately enough, two savages with clubs, and the landholding in 1874 was as follows:–

Edinburgh County—	*Acres.*	*Rental.*
Lord Aberdour	1,500	£7,400
Earl of Morton	8,944	9,041
Fifeshire—		
Lady Aberdour	514	713
Earl of Morton	1,130	2,293
Argyllshire—		
Earl of Morton	46,883	1,685
	58,971	£21,132

THE LORDS OF WEMYSS.

"He maun eat up the sweat and labours of the puir
man's brows . . . But although men wink at this and
ou'rlook it, yet He sits above that sees it."
Charteris, Preface to Lindsay's Works (1568).

NO history at my command gives any indication of the origin of
the Wemyss family. They first appear in Fife as "De Wemyss,"
Sheriffs of Fife, and seem to have taken no royal grant as an insult.
They have never figured prominently in history, and their
acquisitions of land were made so silently and judiciously that the
recorders can only say that the "lands of Luce passed from the
Carlyles to the Wemyss family," or that "Garleton passed into the
family of the Earl of Wemyss."* The present Wemyss estates are
largely the result of two happy marriages, one with the heiress to
the Queensberry lands and the other with the heiress of Colonel
Charteris of Armisfield. The Douglases, of which the Queensberrys
were a branch, I have already written about. The first Duke of
Queensberry, as Lord High Treasurer of Scotland, "raised the wind"
by heavily fining such of the Protestant gentry as did not
wholeheartedly swallow Episcopacy, and the holder of the title in
1747 made extraordinary demands from the Treasury for the
discontinuance of his hereditary jurisdictions, real and supposed.
For Porterston he claimed much and got nothing; for Dalgarno he
claimed £8000 and got £1621; for the Sheriffship of Dumfries he
asked £6000 and got £5000.

Of Colonel Charteris and his estates, Dr. Arbuthnot says,

---

* See Chalmers' "Caledonia."

"without trade or profession, without trust of public money, and without bribe-worthy service, he acquired—or more properly 'created' a ministerial estate. He was the only person of his time who could cheat without the mask of honesty."

The family owned in 1874:–

	Acres.	Gross Annual Rental.
Berwickshire—		
Earl of Wemyss	1,261	£747
Edinburghshire—		
Earl of Wemyss	1,504	5,370
Earl of Wemyss (Mines)	–	200
Fifeshire—		
Erskine Wemyss of Kirkcaldy	6,925	20,806
Haddington—		
Earl of Wemyss	10,140	22,317
Peebles—		
Earl of Wemyss	41,257	14,332
Perthshire—		
Earl of Wemyss	3,010	7,666
	64,097	£71,438

THE MARJORIBANKS.

THE Marjoribanks who first appears in Scots history is the Thomas Marjoribanks, a lawyer, who was Provost of Edinburgh in 1541. They were merely small landholders till about 1795, when one of them appeared prominently in the East India Company, then at the height of its robbery and oppression. This Marjoribanks was twice chairman of the concern, and his son became a partner in Coutts' Bank. The family was now between British "finance" and Indian "misery" exceedingly wealthy, and a Marjoribanks was raised to the peerage in 1866. All the following estates have been paid for:–

Berwickshire—	*Acres.*	*Gross Annual Rental.*
Lady Marjoribanks of Ladykirk	5,853	9,991
Trustees of the late Lord	979	1,763
Inverness-shire—		
Sir Dudley Coutts Marjoribanks	19,186	1,097
	26,018	£12,851

THE KEITHS.

"The Barons of Scotland are now turned masterful
thieves and ruffians, oppressing the poor by violence
and wasting the Church."

Complaint from Abbot of Aberbrothock (1542).

THE first Keith was a foreign pirate, Hervei by name, who entered
the service of David I, and got from him the Manor of Keith, in East
Lothian, from which place the family afterwards took its name. Under
Malcolm IV they became Mareschals of Scotland; in 1178 they
unsuccessfully attempted to steal the patronage of Keith Church;
about 1199 they got large estates in Kincardine by marriage with an
heiress of the Frasers; they sucked in many estates in Aberdeen-shire
during Robert Bruce's time; Inverugie they acquired by marriage
from the Cheynes (who were also Norman pirates), and at Dunotter
for many long years they kept a castle where torture was a common
occurrence, and where, in 1685, some 167 Covenanters, men and
women, were incarcerated for a whole summer in a dark underground
chamber, ankle deep in mire and filthy. There was only standing
room: the Covenanters were subjected to horrible tortures, and many
of them died. The Keiths annexed the "rich temporalities of the
Abbey of Deer" in James VI's time, and in answer to any outraged
public opinion, they calmly retorted—"They say Quhat say they?
They haif said, Let thame say!" Marischal College in Aberdeen is
endowed from part of the stolen Church lands. The Keiths fell with
the Stuart Kings, and in 1874 only possessed:—

	Acres.	Rental.
Aberdeenshire—Earl of Kintore	17,021	£15,801
Kincardineshire—Earl of Kintore	17,370	16,908
	34,391	£32,709

149

There is a fine double *entendre* in the family motto, "Quae Amissa Salva"—what has been lost is safe—and the Abbot of Deer, were he alive to-day, might point a moral from his reading of the text.

THE MONTGOMERIES.

"God keep ill gear out of my hands, for if my hands once get it, my heart will never part with it."
— *"The Earl of Eglinton's Prayer."*
— *Kelly's Collection of Scottish Proverbs.*

THE Montgomeries are descended from a cut-throat called Roger de Mundejumbri, who came over in the train of William the Conqueror in 1066. A descendant of his, finding his way as a hired warrior into Scotland, was given a grant of the lands of Eaglesham by King Malcolm. It was at this time that there "first originated here the idea of exclusive property in land."* In 1360 Sir John Montgomery married himself into the extensive possessions of the Eglintons, which included Ardrossan district, the ancient lands of the Barclays. The title of Winton was added later on by marriage with the Setons. The Eglinton Family seems to have its prosperity fairly safely built on the stolen lands of Kilwinning Abbey. Burke says that the fifth Earl "purchased" the lands in 1594; but this statement is directly contradicted by other and more reliable authorities. Chalmers contradicted by other and more reliable authorities. Chalmers says, "The Earl of Eglinton finally obtained its (Kilwinnning's) various possessions under several grants of the King and Acts of Parliament."†

At the time of the Reformation the Abbey held no fewer than 16 parishes, Tarbolton, Beith, etc., so that a considerable portion of the present Eglinton estates must consist of the plunder

---

* "History of Eglinton and Winton"—Fullarton, p. 21.
† Ibid. Vol. VI., p. 485.

of the ancient Tyronensian Abbey. In 1612 Kilwinning was taken away from the Eglintons for some reason or other, and given to Lord Balfour of Burleigh, who, however, obligingly sold it to Eglinton for 800 merks. Towards the end of the 18th century the Earl of Eglinton removed most of the remains of the walls to Eglinton, possibly to serve utilitarian purposes in building dry-stone dykes, farm steadings etc. At the time of our 1874 Domesday Book the family, omitting smaller owners, laid claim to:–

Ayrshire—	*Acres.*	*Rental.*
Earl of Eglinton	23,585	£32,504
Earl of Eglinton (Harbours)	46	4,525
Earl of Eglinton (Mines)	–	9,520
Buteshire—		
Earl of Eglinton	671	184
Lanarkshire—		
Earl of Eglinton	5,866	4,097
Peebles—		
Montgomery of Stanhope	18,172	6,945
Kinross—		
Montgomery of Stanhope	2,336	3,129
	50,676	60,904

THE BOYLES.

"Clear the way, my lords and lackeys! you have had
your day."   *—Swinburne*

THE Earl of Glasgow holds lands in Scotland as follow:–

	Acres.	*Rental.*
Ayrshire	24,968	£13,855
Ayrshire (Mines)	–	4,503
Dumbartonshire	175	359
Dumbartonshire (Mines)	–	4,205
Buteshire	1,883	1,979
Renfrewshire	4,453	6,811
Renfrewshire (Mines)	–	480
	31,479	£32,192

The family is an extremely old one, and as the "De Boiles" were
certainly settled at Kelburne in the reign of Alexander III, it is
surprising that they, so comparatively insignificant, should have
preserved their estates during all these turbulent centuries. They
do not, any of them, appear to have been engaged in notorious
theft or scandalous murder, and, indeed, with the exception of the
first Earl, who got his titles for his labours in promoting the union
of the Crowns, the Boyles have done little but quietly breed
successors to the privilege of drawing rents. The family motto is
"Dominus Providebit "—The Lord will provide. So far the task
has been undertaken by the working classes of the West of Scotland.

THE DRUMMONDS.

"Satan's soldiers and rotten members."
—*The Abbot of Inchaffray (1490)*.

A HISTORY of the lands presently held in Scotland by Lord Willoughby D'Eresby takes us back curiously enough to no less a personage than Attila, King of the Huns, "The Scourge of God," "The Terror of the World," etc. This gentleman who flourished about A.D.444, made a specialty of ferocity in warfare. He was a fratricide, and died, aged 124, on the very night of his third marriage. He made a brave endeavour to emulate the patriarch Abraham, inasmuch as he left sixty sons, legitimate and otherwise. His daughters have not been estimated by the chroniclers. A descendant of his, Mauritz, a sea captain, commanded the ship that brought over Queen Margaret to marry Malcolm Canmore. For this signal service of ferrying the lady across the water he graciously accepted royal grants of estates which ran from the shores of the Gareloch, across Dumbarton and Stirling, into Perthshire. He was also appointed Thane or Seneschal of Lennox. He took the name of Drummond from the parish of Drymen, and founded a race of inveterate ruffians. In course of time the Priory of Inchmahome (or the "Island of the bell that tolled for mass") was annexed; grants of land in Perthshire were received from Robert the Bruce; and we read that one Brice Drummond lost his life in "encroaching" on the Menteith lands. In Robert II's time they got Auchterarder, Cargill, and Kincardine, all plunder from property of two young heiresses "in the King's gift." About 1490, Lindsay of Pitscottie tells us the Master of Drummond was beheaded for burning to death "six scoir of Murrays" inside the Kirk of Monivaird. Of the ladies of the family, two became King's mistresses, and in the Treasury Accounts 1488-1502, there are many entries showing Kingly gifts from the public pocket to one of them, Lady Margaret.

Here are one or two of the entries:–

"1496—June 9th. Giffen to the Lady Mergret of Drummond £20 0/12d. Sept. 10—To the Lady Lundy for Mergret Drummondis costis 40/."

"1503—10th. February. Item to the priestis that sing in Dumblane for Mergret Drummond, their quarter fee, 5/."

In 1682 the Drummonds collared every office in Scotland worth having. They kept a "private executioner" at Crieff and "preserved their right of pit and gallows" up to 1706. Their power, however, fell with the Stuarts, and the property—which was saved by judiciously taking both sides in the dynastic struggle—has gone by marriage to the D'Eresebys of the English house of Ancaster. Omitting smaller rent-drawers, the family appeared in the 1874 return as follows:–

Perthshire—	*Acres.*	*Gross Annual Rental.*
Drummond of Cromlix	7,465	£4,240
Blair Drummond	13,817	15,409
Drummonds of Buckruthven, Balquhandy, and Megginch	2,509	3,499
Willoughby D'Eresby	76,837	28,955
Stirlingshire—		
Blair Drummond	372	700
Edinburgh—		
Drummond of Hawthornden	482	1,234
	101,482	£51,037

City Treasurers of Glasgow have had bountiful occasion to remember the D'Eresby rapacity that was shown when Loch Katrine had to be tapped for water.

THE ERSKINES.

"The people who, you know, bestow the prize,
To men most worthless, and. Like salves to fame,
With foolish reverence hail a titled name,
And, rapt, with awe-struck admiration gaze
When the long line its images displays."
—*Horatius.*

BEFORE the feudal Earls there were the Celtic Marmaors or Great
Stewards in Scotland, and the country was divided into seven
divisions, over each of which a Marmaor ruled. One of these
divisions was the territory of Mar, stretching from the Don to the
Dee. There were Marmaors of Mar long before the dawn of
authentic history, and the Earldom has since been held by so many
families that one becomes weary as he traces down the centuries
the expulsions, annexations, and royal grants which changed, every
generation or two, the governing family. About 1403 the estates
were held by Sir Malcolm Drummond, brother-in-law of Robert
III, but he was brutally outraged and murdered by the "Wolf of
Badenoch," an illegitimate son of the fourth son of Robert II. Then
the "Wolf" who is one of the most dastardly and cruel scoundrels
in Scots history, and among whose exploits is the burning of Elgin
Cathedral, stormed Kildrummie Castle, and captured Sir Malcolm's
widow. He forced her through sheer terror to marry him and to
hand over the titles and castles in her possession as a "marriage
gift." Finally the estates devolved through marriage on the Erskine
family. The Erskines owed their position to two happy marriages,
one with the Bruces and the other with the Stuarts, and while both
these families held the throne, the Erskines absorbed huge grants

of land. Then finally they married into the Earldom of Mar. The Earldom of Cardross was "granted" them (with estates carved out of the plundered Abbacies of Dryburgh and Cambuskenneth) by James VI, and the ostensible reason for the grant was that Lady Mary Stewart, Mar's *fiancée*, refused to marry him unless he could guarantee her progeny a title. He already owned a family by a former wife, and Lady Mary wanted her own offspring to be as "noble" as her prospective stepchildren. The Erskines were among the most powerful Earls in Scotland until the 1715 Rebellion, when they lost nearly everything through adherence to the Stuarts. The standard of rebellion was raised on the "Braes o' Mar," but the Earl himself was a contemptible cur. When he succeeded to his estates he joined the Whig party, "merely because it was his interest to do so." After getting all he could from the Whigs, he went over to the Tories. Then the Whigs came back to power, and he again became a strenuous Whig. He was by them appointed Secretary for Scotland, and he supported the Union of the Parliaments. He then found this was unpopular in Scotland, so he voted for the dissolution of the Union in the House of Lords. When in 1713 the Whigs lost office, Mar "without shame or scruple" went over to their opponents, again became Secretary of State, and manager of Scotland. "These repeated tergiversations," we are told, "rendered him notorious even among the loose-principled politicians," and he was nick-named "Bobbing John."

When George I came to the throne he showed at first contempt for this human chameleon, and later dismissed him from office. In revenge Mar sent the fiery cross round the Highlands, and began the Rebellion of 1715. He was totally unfit for the enterprise, and after the Battle of Sheriffmuir, bolted for France, "leaving his deluded and indignant followers to shift for themselves."* In Paris he got control of Jacobite affairs, and had the unlimited confidence of James. He, however, for a pension of £2000 to himself and £1500 a year to his wife and daughter, basely betrayed the Jacobites to the Earl of

---

* "The Erskines "—J. Taylor, F.S.A. Vol. II., p. 113.

Stair, who represented the Government. Latterly he was discovered embezzling the Jacobite funds, and was dismissed with ignominy. The title was restored to the family in 1824.

The Earl of Rosslyn, by-the-bye, like a large number of Scots noblemen who do not know much about the history of Scotland, boasts that he is a "Baronet of Nova Scotia." This "honour" is a matter of ridicule to anyone acquainted with the facts of its inception; and were I the Earl of Rosslyn I should be rather ashamed to say anything about it. The simple facts are these. In 1625 the King was short of coin, and hearing of some place called Nova Scotia, he decided, possibly with a keen sense of the humour of the business, to annex it (on paper) to his dominions. He then announced that he had much land to give away—for, of course, a consideration; and as a special inducement to purchasers he would throw a baronetcy into the bargain. Among the noblemen whose greed induced them to stand on the Castle Hill at Edinburgh and go through, what McKerlie, the historian, calls "the farce of infeftment" was an ancestor of the Earl of Rosslyn. He, like the others, paid the King £150, and got in return 6000 paper acres in Nova Scotia and the precious baronetcy.†

In 1874 the family owned:–

	Acres.	Rental.
Clackmannan—		
Earl of Kellie	6,163	£8,256
Earl of Kellie (Mines)	–	1,260
Edinburgh—		
Earl of Rosslyn	99	737
Fifeshire—		
Erskine of Cambo	2,937	6,727
Earl of Kellie	162	331
Earl of Rosslyn	3,221	8,449
Earl of Rosslyn (Mines)	–	1,224
Perthshire—		
Erskine of Kippen	6,245	4,020
	18,827	£31,004

† See also Knight's "England," Vol. III., ch. 22, p. 355.

There are also other smaller septs of the family, holding between them about 20,000 acres, rental £17,000.

James Stuart, first Earl of Moray, was an illegitimate son of James V by a daughter of the fourth Lord Erskine. He was given "the office of Prior of St Andrews" and many baronies and lordships by his Royal father. His descendant, the Earl of Moray, held in 1874:–

	Acres.	Gross Annual Rental.
Fifeshire	7,463	£8,735
Fifeshire (Mines)	–	2,350
Inverness-shire	7,035	5,171
Elgin	21,669	9,420
Perth	40,553	10,800
	76,720	£36,476

Most of the land was originally stolen from the Church. The family motto is "Salus per Christum Redemptorem"—"Salvation through Christ the Redeemer."

THE SEAFIELDS.

IN the Landowners' Return the Earl of Seafield, in whose person is combined the once great families of Ogilvie and Grant, is shown as owner of:–

	Acres.	Rental.
Banff	48,946	£34,268
Elgin	96,721	21,138
Inverness	160,224	16,478
	305,891	£71,884

The earliest Ogilvie on record is one Gilbert, a soldier in William the Lion's time, who somehow got a grant of the lands of Ogilvy and thereafter called himself Gilbert de Ogilvy. In 1437 an Ogilvy married the daughter and heir of Sir John Sinclair of Deskford. Early in the 18th century the estates of Grant and Ogilvy were united by marriage. There has been only one prominent scion of this family, James, the fourth Earl of Findlater, who made his profession the law. He had "a soft tongue," was very greedy, and after amassing a fortune as Chancellor, etc., got himself safely quartered as a pensioner at £3000 per annum on the funds of the Post Office. He was appropriately nicknamed "The Hyena."

THE ELLIOTS.

"In early tribal society chiefs were not hereditary, but elected 'by free suffrage of both males and females of adult age' (p. 72) . . . The oldest tenure by which land was held, was by the tribe in common (p. 541). . . Property and office were the foundations upon which aristocracy planted itself (p. 555)."
—*"Ancient Society," Lewis H. Morgan, LL.D.*

THE Elliots were to the time of the Union of the Crowns a Border clan whose existence depended on a paucity of armed police. Their functions were murder, assault and battery, cattle and hen-stealing, and with the Armstrongs they kept the Borders in a perpetual fever of disturbance by foray and faction.

Originally they were vassals of the Douglases, and resided at Elliot in Fifeshire; but the Earl of Angus, to increase his military importance and prestige, transported them to the Borders. There is abundant testimony that despite their plundering propensities, they held a much higher code of honour than the Norman families who eventually drove them beyond the seas. Bishop Leslie tells us that their word was their bond, and that so far were they from individual greed that they considered each no property as his own, but as belonging to the clan. When the Douglas power was broken, and a settled peace arranged with England, many of the members of the Elliot clan were forcibly transported abroad, while the Chief and his relatives stuck to the home-lands. In 1620*, one hundred and twenty broken men were thus "seized upon and sent abroad."

---

* "The Border Elliots "—G. F. S. Elliot, p. 204.

Many were sent to Ulster and Virginia. Many were hung without trial, and some were hung after a farcical trial; in short, the same cruel ghastly crushing and expropriation of the people took place on the Borders at the beginning of the 17th century as took place a century and a century and a half later in the Highlands. The Earl of Minto is descended from these Elliot chiefs. His family success is due to the Sir Gilbert Elliot who took a prominent part in the Revolution of 1688 which brought William and Mary to the throne. Sir Gilbert was appointed a Lord of Session with the title of Lord Minto. His son succeeded to his legal offices, and his grandson became Treasurer of the Navy. The family fortunes have been largely augmented by marriages, and in recent years the Lords of Minto have appeared mostly in the second-rate fields of diplomacy, militarism, and politics. One of the daughters of the family, Jane Elliot, wrote the beautiful "Flowers of the Forest," and the present Lord Minto is busy in India suspending the Indian equivalent to the Habeus Corpus Act, and transporting without trial and without indictment peaceable Indian gentlemen, who it is alleged, *might* conceivably one day oppose the continuance of British dominion.

	Acres.	Rental.
Fifeshire—		
Earl of Minto	2,930	2,596
Earl of Minto (Mines)	–	2,804
Roxburgh—		
Elliott of Stobs	16,475	8,934
Elliott of Stobs	2,870	2,575
Elliotts of Kelso, Wolfelee, and Harwood	13,188	9,841
Earl Minto	8,633	6,888
Selkirk —		
Earl Minto	1,032	264
	45,128	£33,902

THE BENTINCKS.

"Deer forest rents come from the rich, but where do the riches of the rich come from? There is only one possible source—from the toiling millions defrauded of the fruits of their toil."
    —*"Men or Deer": W. MacCombie Smith, F.S.A.*

THE Bentincks are of no later date than the last German invasion, one of them coming across with William, Prince of Orange as a page-boy. I am not now concerned with the English landed families, and consequently I must only recommend any one who wishes to study the history of the rapacious Bentincks to Mr. Howard Evans' "Our Old Nobility"; but while it is necessary here to state that part of the Scots estates was got by marriage with the heiress of the last General Scott, and part was honestly purchased, the Bentinck fortunes (and consequently the wherewithal to purchase Scots deer forests) are the result of the most shameless Court begging and sycophant greed to be found anywhere in British annals. The brazen-faced Dutch favourite begged for Crown lands, and the king willingly gave, even although from an outraged people and Parliament there arose clamant and spirited protests. With the spoil from these English Crown lands, the Bentincks have afforested huge lands in Caithness. Langwell was afforested for deer in 1864, and Braemore was purchased and afforested for the same purpose in 1880. Here are 63 square miles from which our hardiest stocks have been expelled in order that an idle descendant of a Court beggar shall breed and slaughter deer. The Duke of Portland is of course a patriot, and believes earnestly in encouraging the expropriated peasant to fight in defence of his (the Duke's) deer forests, should some filibustering German attack them from an airship. But when the people really do begin to fight for their native land, it will be the present Dutch and Norman land-grabbers they will smack first. Potential buccaneers can be dealt with afterwards.

Ayrshire	*Acres.*	*Rental.*
Duke of Portland	24,787	£33,625
Duke of Portland (Harbour)	64	10,708
Duke of Portland (Mines)	–	16,199
Caithness—		
Duke of Portland	81,605	7,902
	106,456	£68,434

THE HOPES.

"It is a shamefull thing that the privat gayne of some two or three persons sould be putt in balance with the weele of this whole yle."

—*King James VI.*

"Let God but grant me life and there shall not be a spot in my dominion where the key shall not keep the lock and the furze bush the cow, though I myself could lead the life of a dog to accomplish it."

—*King James I.*

THERE exists even to this day in the Leadhills a tradition that the mines there are common property. But I have searched diligently all the records and charters accessible to me, and I am afraid I can find no more legal justification for the common ownership of the Leadhills than there is for all hills—lead and otherwise—in Scotland. Originally all the lands in Scotland were owned by the clans and tribes who inhabited them. When central authority developed, all lands gradually became vested in the Crown, in theory at least, for the common weal. The Leadhills, like other hills, were once common property, then they became Crown property, and latterly they passed, as did other lands, from the Crown to private interests. But the Leadhills have a peculiar history of their own, and as the fortunes of the Hope family have been largely built on the metals won from these upland wastes, and as the labour of generations of Leadhills miners has reared Lord Linlithgow to his present exalted position, I may be pardoned for a remark or two on the history of the "Hills."

In 1576, Thomas Foulis, an Edinburgh goldsmith, got a patent from the Scots Parliament "to adventure and search for gold and silver mines" in the Leadhills. For this purpose he employed a Flemish prospector called Bulmer. In three years £100,000 of gold was produced; but the works appear to have been discontinued when the workmen demanded the living wage of fourpence per day! Bulmer died in poverty, though Foulis waxed fat, and latterly in 1592 is said to have leased for 21 years the lands in which the mines lay. This Act of 1592, referred to more particularly in the appendix, instituted actual and literal slavery among the miners. In 1637 Anne Foulis was left "sole heiress"—which fact shows that the 21 years had already somehow stretched themselves out—and was engaged in a lawsuit about titles. Her advocate was a young lawyer called James Hope, who after winning the case, took care also to win the heiress. In 1661 an Act was passed "granting" the mines to (Sir) James Hope, who also contrived to secure the Governorship of the Mint; but the King made an important stipulation, viz.:–

> "The King takes the miners under his special protection, and exempts them from all taxes, both in peace and war." *

The miners were, however, practically slaves; they could not leave the mines; and heavy penalties were imposed on anyone who should "intromit" with them, without a pass from Sir James Hope. Since that charter was granted, the Hopes have drawn enormous fortunes from the mines, even if the poor miners do not appear to have fared so well. Says Miss Martineau, writing in 1852:–

> "Looking round on the very small cabbage patches of the miners, remembering their oatmeal diet, without even a smell of bacon to their bread, pondering also the average of 9/ a week, which leaves so many with only 6/, we inquired whether poaching could in such a wild scene be kept within bound. The answer was that the poacher would forfeit everything if de-

---

* "God's Treasure House in Scotland "—Porteous, p. 67.

> tected. It is wonderful, and must be the strong com-
> pulsion of circumstances that hungering men can see
> . . . and can abstain from taking."

Precisely at what period the Hopes, despite the original charter, managed to get the people induced to pay taxes and rates I cannot discover, but the miners were certainly paying poor's rate in 1873, and school rate in 1876; every miner, married or single, being rated at 1/8 per quarter for school fees. At Leadhills the curfew still "tolls the knell of parting day," and there appears to be a remnant of the ancient communal privileges still surviving. At anyrate, they were surviving till a very recent period. The miners in their spare time have reclaimed much hill land (394 acres by 1876), and some hundred of them possess cows which are looked after by herd-boys, "who are fed by the owners in turn." Cottages built by the miners are held rent free, though all property is legally held without lease at the pleasure of the Marquis of Linlithgow. This is a most—to put it mildly—unsatisfactory tenure; and with the memory of the robbing of Wanlockhead still fresh, the Leadhills miners would be well advised to consider carefully their position. Up till 1842 Wanlockhead was a thriving, happy village. If a man reclaimed waste land or built a cottage, it was his own, and could be sold or left to his descendants. Then the Buccleugh Family acquired the estate, and the miners were legally informed,† "that whatever privileges they enjoyed under the Marquis of Bute, the same would they possess under his Grace of Buccleugh. This document, unfortunately, was lost, and then:–

> "First, sanction was required as to the party coming
> into possession, and eventually when the key or the
> land was required, it had to be given up otherwise
> employment ceased . . . little or no land has since then
> been reclaimed, many have been disheartened or left."

Just so! It is the old, old story, and it bears a pointed moral to the "small owners" of cottages in Leadhills.

---

† Ibid, p. 122

The Hopes have not swaggered much in history, being mostly content to practise punctuality in quietly drawing rents. Niddry was purchased from Lord Wintoun (1678), and Abercorn from Sir Walter Seton. The Annandale estates were secured by marriage; and altogether the land holding totalled in 1874 as follows:–

	Acres.	*Rental.*
Dumfriesshire (Earl of Hopetoun)	2,549	£634
Fifeshire (Earl of Hopetoun)	941	1,717
Haddingtonshire (Earl of Hopetoun)	7,967	15,369
Haddingtonshire (Mines)	–	128
Lanarkshire (Earl of Hopetoun)	19,180	3,246
Lanarkshire (Earl of Hopetoun, Mines)	–	2,246
Linlithgow (Earl of Hopetoun)	11,870	19,018
Linlithgow (Earl of Hopetoun, Mines)	–	1,600
	42,507	£43,958

Jointly with others the Earl owns also 700 acres in Linlithgow, rental £1130, and there are other Hopes drawing £33,000 annually from 7569 acres.

The present Marquis of Linlithgow cannot be a popular figure among Tory politicians, for his recent conduct in refusing to part with Rosyth, unless at a scandalous price, cast odium on the whole landlord class. It will be remembered that Mr. Balfour's administration required Rosyth as a Naval base. The land was 1200 acres in extent plus 300 acres of foreshore: the whole 1500 acres being rated to produce £1700 annual rent. But the Marquis actually refused to let the land go *at less than £139,000 or 80 years' purchase.*

Of course, the government was forced to accept his terms— it required the land in question for a Naval base, and they were helpless while this Tory "patriot" taking advantage of the robber rules, miscalled Land Laws, made by himself and his friends, turned our national necessity to his private gain.

APPENDIX.

ON THE TWO HUNDRED YEARS SLAVERY IN SCOTLAND

So far as I can gather, *Neyfship* or Serfdom seems to have died out in Scotland towards the end of the 14th Century, the last proved claim on record being made on the year 1364. This would make Scotland the first country in Europe to purge itself of the chain-gang-lash-chattel institution, which as everybody knows, persisted in a peculiarly obnoxious form in the semi-civilised States of America right down to the period of the Civil War. But if *Neyfship* had gone, compulsory service and vassalage remained for several centuries; and, indeed slavery itself re-appeared in 1606, and the miners and salt-workers from that date till 1799 were bought and sold as part and parcel of the pits in which they were condemned to work for life.

I have, in searching old records for the histories appearing on preceding pages, frequently come across traces and evidences of this slavery period, and it is perhaps as well that a few of these evidences should be preserved.

Land in Scotland was until comparatively recent times sold *cum nativis* (with natives), and although some nefs or slaves were slaves astricted to a particular piece of land, others were slaves by birth, and could be transferred or sold away from lands on which they were born. In William the Lion's time one proprietor could sell to another the person of a peasant born on his territory, with all his children. Here is a copy of a charter dated in the year 1178:–

CHARTER.

"Richard of Morville, Constable to the King of Scots,
to all his worthy men and friends present and to come.
Greeting—Know ye that I have given and quit claimed

and by this charter confirmed to Henry of St. Clair
for three merks, which he gave me, Edmund, the son
of Bonda and Gallimichael, his brother and their sons
and daughters, and whole progeny, descending from
them, loosed and freed from me and my heirs, to him
and his heirs, on the condition that if it shall happen
that they in any event go away from the aforesaid
Henry, that is with his permission and goodwill, it
shall not be lawful for them to pass over into the dominion of another master, or to any other than myself and to my land."

In our "National MSS." (Part I., No. 54) there is a deed of sale
by which a Berwickshire laird sells to the priory of Coldingham,
a serf, named Turkill Hog, and his sons and daughters, the
whole family being equal in value to 3 merks. But this form
of slavery, as I have already said, died out, and it is not until
the year 1606 that bondage in its worst form began.

In early times, landowners had worked their mines with their
own estate labourers, and wages were paid partly in cash
and partly in produce; but with the increased demand for
coal—chiefly for export purposes—there arose a large demand for outside labour, and fees and bounty money were
freely offered to induce fresh labour to the mines. To regu-
late (so it is said) this competition for labourers, Parliament
passed in 1606 an Act ordaining that no miner could be
employed without a testimonial from his last employer, and
that a miner who left his work without leave could be claimed
within a year and a day by the employer if that gentleman
discovered him. Colliery owners or their agents were heavily fined if discovered "intromitting" with the miners in another mine, and finally, *mine owners were empowered to appre-
hend vagabonds and sturdy beggars and set them to labour in the
mines.* Thereafter these apprehended workmen could not
leave without the master's consent, and became regarded as
part of the property of the mine.

The Act of 1614 gave the mine-owner additional powers.
He could impose fines at sweet will, withhold wages, seques-
trate goods, suspend from employment, and punish his miners "in their personis by scourging, laying in the stockis, or

lang imprisonment," (Records of Mining in Scotland, Cochrane Patrick.) and so as late as 1771, said Mr. Jas. Barrowman, M.E. Secretary of the Mining Institute of Scotland, in a recent lecture, *"The value of forty good colliers, with their wives and children, was estimated to be worth £4,000, or £100 each family. It was customary for parents to bind their children in a formal manner to the work, by receiving a gift from the master on the occasion of the baptism of the children."* You will observe the complicity of the Church in these transactions. But not only had the colliers entered the state of slavery: all other workers in connection with the pits, and all workers engaged in the salt-works—"salters" as they were called— were also in literal bondage, and an Act of 1701 reforming criminal procedure (our Scots Habeus Corpus Act) expressly excludes colliers and salters from its benefits. There is evidence, too, in the records of these early times that the question of miners' holidays exercised our governors. In 1641 it seems the miners took "French leave" at "Pasche, Yoole, and Witsonday," and at other times "to the great offence of God and prejudice of their maisteris," and so a compulsory "six-days' week" was instituted, with a penalty for non-observance of "twentie shillings for everie day . . . and other punishment for thaire bodies."

There was no limit to the snivelling, hypocritical cant with which these mine-owners and their legal servants justified these atrocities. A memorial, dated 1682, declares with grief that "many hundreds of poore people are forced to betake themselves to foreigne plantations, where sometimes they learne those damnable prineciples of phanaticism," and we learn this "might in some measure be prevented by good laborious works underground."

Hugh Miller gives us a striking description (quoted in "Sketches of Early Scotch History."— Cosmo Innes, p.499.) of a slave village in the immediate vicinity of Niddry Mill, near Edinburgh. The houses were a "wretched assemblage of dingy, low-roofed, tile-covered hovels." The collier women, "poor, over-toiled creatures," carried all the coal up a long turnpike stair, inserted in one of the shafts, and it was calculated that each day's labour was equivalent to carrying a hundredweight from the sea level to the top of Ben Lomond.

No wonder, poor things, "they cried like children under their load," no wonder "a peculiar type of mouth . . . wide, open, thick-lipped, projecting equally above and below . . . like savages," was developed, but it is a matter for extreme wonderment that this sort of thing should be going on in Scotland at the very time our sapient legislators were making St. Stephens ring with denunciation for negro slavery.

This scandalous state of affairs continued down to the year 1799, but it is evident that there must have been emancipation agitations of some sort considerably prior to that date, for in the year 1774 an Act was passed providing cumbrous, costly, and ineffective machinery by which the miner if wealthy enough to take legal process, could attain his freedom. An interesting fact about the Act of 1799 is that it incidentally brought the first Miners' Union into being. When the Bill was going through Parliament the miners heard that even this new Emancipation Act was to be burdened by what they considered vicious Clauses; and so some 500 of them in Lanarkshire banded themselves together, subscribed two shillings per head, invited the co-operation of all other Scots miners, and sent a Glasgow lawyer to London to do whatsoever he could to get the vicious Clauses withdrawn. This Union, of course, was only a temporary affair, called into being for a particular purpose, and the first real Union with a solid base, "The United Liberal Union of the Operative Colliers and Miners of Scotland," was not formed until the Combination Laws were abolished in 1824. This new Union, by limitation of output, etc., quickly raised wages to the then fabulous sum of ten shillings per day, but reprisals quickly followed, and the mine-owners succeeded in importing large numbers of labourers, mostly Irish, who not only changed the *calibre* and character of the mining districts, but succeeded in reducing wages as well.

Later Acts, the Act of 1842, for instance, which prohibited females and boys under ten years of age, from working underground, considerably raised the status of mining, and the Miners' Unions and Parliamentary action have raised it still further, but much still remains to be done, and it will require to be done in the future as in the past, in the face of bitter hostility from our land and mine-owners.   T. J.